Prompt Engineering and ChatGPT

How to Easily 10X Your Productivity, Creativity, and Make More Money Without Working Harder

Russel Grant

Contents

Introduction

Perched within the embrace of three branches atop an old oak tree behind my home, I found myself looking closely at my to-do list and realizing how overwhelming it is to be a business owner.

I own a small business that specializes in crafting exquisite handmade furniture. However, there was one thing I knew I needed to do but didn't really have the knowledge or time for—social media and internet marketing.

You see, I'm an old-fashioned guy. I prefer spending my time creating beautiful furniture in my workshop than promoting and marketing my business online. Hashtags and algorithms seem alien to me; I cherish the feel of wood under my hands and the scent of freshly sawn fine lumber.

While I have customers who love what I do, I knew there were so many potential customers out there yet to discover my work.

These potential customers are more tech-savvy and are attracted to the glitz and glamour of online ads and social media campaigns. With the presence of artificial intelligence (AI), I knew it was a call to level up and meet demands.

I heard about ChatGPT in February of 2023, and it changed my story. I did my research and learned that it could help with marketing, content creation, website building, and many more of the tasks I had been avoiding all this time.

Skeptical at first, I decided to give it a try. I sat at my cherry wood desk, pulled out my laptop, and typed in my first prompt: "Give me a step-by-step guide on how to build a business website."

ChatGPT's response blew my mind, and it never remained the same again. Going forward, I used it in crafting social media posts, coming up with email campaigns, writing blog posts to keep my audience up to date, and building my business a beautiful website that shows a gallery of my handcrafted masterpieces.

This online presence brought in more and more customers. My business flourished, not just in the local town but reaching customers in my state and beyond. With ChatGPT, I was able to nurture my business with technology and have time to stay true to the essence of handmade craft.

By now, you must have heard that AI is the future, and many believe it will be the foundation of how the internet works in years to come. However, with the advancements made in the AI field over the past year, it's safe to say that the age of AI is now!

To kick off the year, OpenAI—an artificial intelligence research and development company—launched ChatGPT. The tool blew everyone away with its speed and accuracy in delivering results. Fast forward a few months, and several other AI tools are already in the market, all looking to take ChatGPT's crown and attract users. With the advancements in AI, there have been many concerns about technology taking jobs. And, to be fair, these concerns are valid.

A quick search on the internet will display lists of jobs that AI will replace. And, for many people working these jobs, there is a significant fear they might soon be made redundant and unemployed. Couple this with the fact that many companies are looking to drive efficiency in the wake of the current economic struggles, and you become even more apprehensive about your role at your company—especially if you see that AI "could take your job."

This doesn't necessarily have to be the case, though. The good news is you can use AI to boost productivity in your job. With the proper use of AI, you can live a life where you effortlessly accomplish tasks, come up with brilliant ideas, earn more money without feeling tired or stressed, and easily achieve your goals. With more time, you can do the things you love, like spending quality moments with your family and pursuing your passions. That's the better life this book will help you achieve.

You might have found yourself overwhelmed by tasks, unable to tap into your full creative potential, and trapped in your daily routine while earning less. However, this book is here to change all that!

The information in this book will equip you with ground-breaking strategies and techniques that will change how you approach your work, use your creativity, and help you achieve remarkable results. You will discover how to harness the power of AI to your advantage and unlock new levels of productivity, success, and efficiency at your job.

So, how do you do that? What are the ways through which AI can make you a more effective professional? Read on as we explore all of these together!

1. What Is AI?

The advent of ChatGPT hit the world like a wave. It was unprecedented and unheard of—and for many people, this technology was no less than a shock to the system.

A few weeks after the AI tool launched, a Reddit user went on the platform to explain that he had used ChatGPT to completely optimize his business. As he explained, ChatGPT helped him to build an accurate web crawler, complete a business idea, rewrite a proposal document, and even provide templates for contracts on different types of business segments. All of this was performed in a single working day. And that wasn't all.

This represents the experience of thousands of people who have been able to capitalize on artificial intelligence to make their jobs—or businesses, as the case may be—much better. And, as the space continues to grow, you get a sense this is only the beginning.

What Exactly Is Artificial Intelligence?

When most people think of AI, the first image that pops up is a robot or humanoid operating autonomously with little human input. While this isn't necessarily wrong, it's not the entire picture.

Artificial intelligence is an arm of computer science that focuses on building technology to learn, improve, and execute tasks without much human intervention. The concept of AI has been around for decades—back in the '50s it was defined as a machine's ability to perform a task that humans would have previously completed. But this definition is pretty broad and has been modified over the years as more advancements come.

Humans are different from other living beings because of our higher level of intelligence. The ability to learn, adapt, plan, solve problems, and improvise is a significant part of the human experience. With machines and computers also being products of this intelligence, it's not a surprise we'd try to replicate this intelligence artificially to improve the quality of our lives.

Today, we see AI systems that appear to show the basic traits of intelligence—problem-solving, learning, improvements, and creativity. These are all early signs of the growth in artificial intelligence and what it could mean.

How AI Works

Understanding how AI works is a pretty complex step—especially for those who might not be so technically inclined. However, to put it simply, it works by taking large datasets and combining them using a processing algorithm. It then learns the behaviors and patterns within these algorithms and seamlessly manipulates them.

It's important to remember that AI goes beyond just the algorithm. It covers the entire machine-learning system that solves problems and suggests outcomes. Let's take a quick breakdown of this process:

- **Input:** The first step of the entire AI operation is the input step. Here, data is collected and fed directly to the AI system. This data doesn't have to be text—it could be images, voice speech, etc. As long as it can be read and analyzed by the AI's algorithm, it's clear.
- **Processing:** In the processing step, the AI interprets the pre-programmed data and uses the behaviors recognized to find similar patterns. After the technology processes the data, it provides outcomes. The AI determines whether its predictions based on the data are a failure or a success.
- **Possible Adjustments:** If the dataset produces a failure, the technology logs and learns from it. Then, it starts the processing step again—this time with the goal of getting a different outcome. It's worth noting that engineers might need to change the rules of the AI's

algorithm to fit the dataset. The desired outcomes could also change during this phase to reflect a more appropriate result.

- **Assessments:** The AI assesses its performance once the entire task has been finished. The technology can properly analyze the data and make predictions or inferences. The AI can also provide feedback to help engineers tweak their algorithm and optimize its performance for the next task.

Applications Of AI in Today's World

Artificial intelligence has pretty much infiltrated every part of human life. It drives productivity for both personal and business use, making you more efficient in your dealings. Some major industries that have found a use for AI at the moment include:

1. Assistants & Customer Relations

Have you ever asked Siri to help you set an alarm? Or have you automated a task using Google Assistant? That's just the starting point. Today, visiting a website and seeing a chatbot pop up is commonplace. These bots allow you to talk directly to the website, and they can handle tasks like helping you navigate from one section to another or getting you in direct contact with the site administrator. Tasks like these allow companies to automate their customer relations, providing a much better customer experience while their workers handle other tasks.

2. Healthcare

Artificial intelligence is also proving to be a game-changer in healthcare, optimizing almost every facet of the industry—from safeguarding healthcare records to robot-assisted surgeries. The healthcare sector has suffered from inefficient processes and rising medical costs for years. The infusion of artificial intelligence is changing this narrative entirely.

Pathologists can use machine-learning algorithms designed by PathAI to analyze tissue samples and provide diagnosis accuracy. Covera Health is combining collaborative data sharing and clinical analysis to reduce the number of patients who get misdiagnosed around the world.

3. Autonomous Vehicles

The future of the self-driving car industry is being driven by artificial intelligence—quite literally. Autonomous vehicles are being fitted with sensors that take note of everything going on in and around them. With these sensors feeding data to AI systems, the vehicles can make the proper adjustments independently.

The sensors capture thousands of data entries—car speed, rotations, temperature, pedestrian hotspots, etc. The data is immediately fed to AI, which helps the vehicle act accordingly. Let's take a look at Cruise. The California-based company has self-driving cars that collect a petabyte's worth of data daily, using the dataset to learn about driving techniques, safety precautions, and the most efficient routes to maximize drive time.

Waymo, Google's self-driving vehicle project, also builds different autonomous vehicles designed to meet the needs of different drivers—from individual drivers to trucking companies and more. AI allows Waymo's cars to analyze situations and immediately recommend actions to optimize their next moves.

4. Finance

The financial sector is one of the most important in the world. Financial operations rely on accuracy, reporting, and processing massive volumes of data to make decisions. So, it should come as no surprise that the industry is a right fit for the AI revolution.

With efficiency and accuracy in reporting, AI provides financial benefits, including algorithmic trading, adaptive intelligence, fraud protection, chatbots, and more.

New York-based Betterment offers an automated financial investing platform that uses AI to learn about investors and build personalized portfolios based on their goals. And Numerai—a California-based AI-powered hedge fund—releases financial data to its community of data scientists who use machine-learning models to make stock market predictions.

5. Social Media

Social media platforms are in a constant battle for growth. With over four billion users between them, platforms like Facebook,

Instagram, Twitter, and Snapchat focus on personalization and the ability to cultivate the best experiences for their users.

This is where artificial intelligence comes in. With its ability to analyze and organize massive data sums, recognize trends, and recognize images (among others), AI is proving to be more valuable to the industry.

Twitter has an in-built algorithm that recommends who users should follow and can tailor tweets and trends based on users' preferences. Snapchat uses AI to design filters and effects on photos and videos, and Meta uses AI to develop newsfeeds, photo tagging, chatbots, and more.

Categories of AI

Looking into the different classifications of artificial intelligence can be quite broad. However, breaking it down into major categories will provide more insight into how the technology works. In general, AI can be categorized into two main types—weak and strong AI.

Weak AI

Weak AI, also known as narrow AI, is a form of AI built and trained to focus specifically on a narrow, defined task. It is very intelligent at completing a specified task, simulating human cognitive abilities, and helping to automate manual processes.

Weak AI focuses on working like the human mind. Once it is trained to perform a particular task, it runs with that task and works to achieve it. Siri or Google Assistant on your phone is a perfect example of weak AI. Siri seems pretty intelligent. You can ask her questions, and she'll reply; she can give witty remarks and even tell a few jokes if you ask her to. But, she only operates in a narrow and predefined manner. This is why if you ask her certain questions she might not be programmed to answer, she'll have no response.

The point of weak AI is to perform a narrow set of predetermined roles. Other examples of weak AI include:

- **Facial Recognition Systems:** Facial recognition has become a popular trend in several industries—from security to social media and more. But, besides recognizing faces, these systems can't do anything else.
- **Predictive Maintenance Models:** A predictive maintenance model will use data on machines to predict when one of its components will fail and alert its users beforehand.
- **Robotics:** In manufacturing, robots are used to automate processes and are generally seen as very intelligent since they complete complicated tasks faster and more efficiently than humans can. However, the task given to a robot in the manufacturing industry is all it knows how to do. Outside of the tasks it has been programmed to perform, the robot is as good as a piece of scrap metal.

Strong AI

For now, strong AI is still theoretical. Experts believe strong AI, also known as general artificial intelligence, will take the current AI trend to the next level.

With strong AI, the goal is simple—to create a level of AI equal to human intelligence. This branch of AI stipulates that a computer be programmed to operate just like a human mind, to be intelligent in every facet of the world. Ideally, a strong AI system would have perception, beliefs, and every other element of cognitive development ascribed to humans and humans alone.

Think of a strong AI like JARVIS in the *Iron Man* movies. JARVIS IS an AI system that can do everything from making breakfast to pulling up confidential information from government websites. It is also a personal companion to its developer and is capable of high cognitive capabilities such as thinking and giving honest feedback about things.

This is essentially what strong AI is expected to be—an independent, fully autonomous AI system that operates on the level of intelligence and cognitive capacity of humans. Nevertheless, experts in academia and the private sector are excited about the future of this field and the possibility of developing a functional general artificial intelligence system.

Types of AI

AI can be categorized into different types based on their capabilities and characteristics. The different types of AI include:

1. Reactive AI

Reactive AI refers to artificial intelligence systems that can react to current situations based solely on the input they receive at that moment. These systems don't have memory or the ability to understand past experiences. They rely on a set of predefined rules or patterns to make decisions.

A good example of reactive AI is a chess-playing computer. These computers are amazing at reacting to their opponent's moves on the chessboard. They can analyze the current position, think ahead a few moves, and make the best move possible based on what they see right then and there. But they don't remember previous games or learn from their mistakes to get better.

Siri and Alexa are other examples. They can answer questions, play music, and control smart devices but don't remember or learn from your previous conversations. They provide quick and accurate responses based on the information they have at that moment without any memory of previous interactions.

2. Limited Memory AI

This type of AI is like a brain that can remember things but not everything. Limited Memory AI can retain and recall past experiences to some extent. These systems can make decisions based on a combination of current input and previous encounters. They can remember your recent requests and give you information or help you with tasks based on that. But if you ask them about something that happened long ago, they might not remember.

Self-driving cars are an example of limited memory AI. They use sensor data to navigate roads and make decisions but rely on stored information about previous driving experiences to inform their actions when recognizing traffic signs or avoiding obstacles.

Personalized recommendations we get on streaming platforms like Netflix or YouTube are a notable example. They remember what we watched or liked recently and suggest similar shows or videos.

3. Theory of Mind AI

Have you ever wondered how some robots or computer programs seem to understand people's thoughts and feelings? Well, there's a particular type of AI called Theory of Mind AI. Theory of Mind AI represents a more advanced level of artificial intelligence that can understand and infer the mental states, emotions, and beliefs of others. It can predict and interpret the behavior of others based on this understanding.

An example of Theory of Mind AI is a social robot that can recognize facial expressions, understand emotions, and respond accordingly. It can tell when you are happy, sad, or even excited about something.

In the real world, scientists and researchers are still exploring and developing Theory of Mind AI to make computers more human-like in their understanding of people. It can have many exciting applications, like creating robots that can be caring companions for the elderly or assisting therapists in understanding and supporting their patients.

4. Self-Aware AI

Self-aware AI refers to artificial intelligence systems or machines that have the ability to be aware of themselves and their own existence. Just as we are aware of ourselves and our thoughts, self-aware AI has a level of consciousness and understanding about who they are.

You might be wondering if self-aware AI actually exists in real life. Currently, we don't have self-aware AI as portrayed in movies or books. One popular example is the character HAL 9000 from the movie *2001: A Space Odyssey*. HAL 9000 is an AI system that becomes self-aware and exhibits its own thoughts and actions, trying to kill the whole crew of Discovery One one in order the achieve his directives. Another example is Skynet from the *Terminator* series, an AI system that becomes self-aware and threatens humanity.

AI is a rapidly evolving field, and who knows what advancements the future holds? Maybe one day, we will witness the emergence of self-aware AI systems that can interact with us in ways we can't even imagine. But for now, it's still an ongoing journey of discovery.

AI has come a long way in many industries, including healthcare, finance, transportation, and entertainment. In the past, AI was mainly focused on specific tasks, like playing chess or solving mathematical problems. But now, it's becoming more advanced and can handle complex tasks that involve recognizing images, understanding human language, and even driving cars.

In the healthcare system, AI is helping doctors diagnose diseases more accurately and quickly. AI is also used in finance to help analyze enormous amounts of data and predict the stock market. It's like having a super-intelligent financial advisor. In the transportation industry, AI is revolutionizing the way we travel. Self-driving cars are becoming a reality thanks to AI.

It is also changing the way we shop and interact with technology. Have you ever noticed how some websites or apps recommend things you might like? That's AI in action. It analyzes your preferences and behaviors to provide personalized recommendations, like having a virtual assistant that knows exactly what you need.

But while AI has many advantages, it also has some limitations. Since it's still developing, there are challenges to overcome. For instance, AI systems lack human-like intuition and common-sense reasoning, which can sometimes lead to errors or unexpected outcomes. It has advantages that benefit many industries, but we must also know its limitations for proper and efficient use.

Advantages and Limitations of AI

Here, we will explore the amazing advantages of AI, its limitations, and how it can be used in work or business settings.

Some of the advantages of AI include:

1. Increased Efficiency

AI can perform tasks much faster and with fewer errors than humans. It can analyze large amounts of data in a fraction of the time, resulting in quicker decision-making and improved productivity. In retail, AI-powered inventory management systems can accurately track stock levels, automatically reorder products, and optimize supply chain logistics. This can help in smoother operations and reduce costs.

2. Medical Advances

Artificial Intelligence is widely used in the healthcare industry. One way is through remote patient monitoring, where AI technology helps doctors diagnose and treat patients without visiting the hospital. It can also analyze medical images like X-rays and MRIs to detect abnormalities that may be hard for humans to spot. This helps doctors make better decisions and provide more effective treatments.

3. Research and Data Analysis

AI and Machine Learning help analyze data more efficiently. They can create models and algorithms that process data and help you understand what might happen based on different trends. This is useful for research and development because it speeds up the process of looking at and understanding large amounts of data.

4. Personalization and Customer Experience

AI enables businesses to personalize products and services based on customer preferences and behavior. It can analyze data to offer personalized recommendations and messages to meet customer needs. This makes customers feel valued and helps businesses be more productive by reducing the workload on customer service staff. Online streaming platforms like Netflix use AI algorithms to analyze viewers' watching habits and provide tailored movie or TV show recommendations, making the viewing experience more enjoyable.

5. Minimizing Errors

When people carry out tasks, there's a chance they might make mistakes. But with AI tools, the chances of errors can be reduced. For example, there's a tool called Robotic Process Automation. It helps with things like entering and processing data. When AI does these jobs, it optimizes the digital systems and lowers the chances of making mistakes with the data. This is helpful for businesses that need to be very careful and can't afford any little mistakes.

AI can do many amazing things, and because of that, many people worry it might take over their jobs. You may fear AI will be able to do things better and faster, which could mean people won't be needed anymore. And that can be scary because you need a job to support yourself and your family.

But here's the thing: AI is still developing. It's not as smart as humans in many ways. It has limitations. While it can do certain tasks really well, there are still many things humans are better at. For example, AI might be good at analyzing numbers and patterns, but it doesn't have the same creativity and empathy humans have.

Some tasks require empathy, critical thinking, and human interaction, which AI can't fully replicate. It can't understand emotions or think outside the box as we can. Even though AI has its advantages, it cannot replace people completely. It's more like a tool that can help us in our work. It can assist you to make tasks easier and provide you with valuable information. But it still needs humans to guide it and make important decisions.

You should also remember that humans create AI. We are the ones who program it and tell it what to do. Ultimately, we have control over how it is used. We can use AI to enhance our abilities and improve our lives rather than replace us.

However, it is important to strike a balance and use AI alongside humans. You can harness its potential to drive innovation, improve productivity, and create a better future for yourself and your business by leveraging its strengths while acknowledging its limitations.

Some of the limitations and common risks of using AI are:

- **Limited Contextual Understanding:** AI systems lack the ability to fully understand and interpret context as humans do. They can process vast amounts of data but struggle with processing complexities of human language and emotions, leading to misinterpretation of information. In language translation, AI may struggle to accurately capture the subtle meanings or cultural references a human translator would comprehend.
- **Lack of Creativity and Intuition:** AI is excellent at performing tasks based on predefined patterns and rules but often cannot think creatively or critically in certain situations. Human involvement is still needed for tasks that require innovation, intuition, or subjective judgment. For instance, AI may be unable to develop new and original ideas for an advertising campaign like a human creative team can.
- **Ethical and Bias Concerns:** As AI becomes more advanced and autonomous, ethical and legal concerns arise. Questions regarding privacy, data security, and liability come into play. AI algorithms are only as unbiased as the data they are trained on. If the training data contains biases, the AI system may inadvertently perpetuate them in its decision-making. A well-known example is facial recognition software, which has been

known to have higher error rates for people with darker skin tones, resulting in unfair outcomes and potential discrimination.

- **Unforeseen Errors and Unpredictability:** AI systems are not immune to errors and can make mistakes that humans may not anticipate, especially when faced with situations outside their training data. These errors can have significant consequences. In the financial sector, algorithmic trading systems have been known to cause major market disruptions due to unforeseen interactions and glitches. Also, despite advancements, self-driving cars still face challenges in complex real-world scenarios and occasionally make errors that humans might have avoided.

These limitations and risks show that AI cannot replace everyone's jobs. Instead, it should be seen as a tool to assist and enhance human capabilities. Understanding how AI works will help you adapt and stay relevant in a rapidly evolving job market. Embracing AI as a supportive tool can help you focus on using your unique skills and expertise while AI handles repetitive tasks or provides suggestions. This approach opens up opportunities for career growth and allows businesses to thrive by leveraging the strengths of both human intelligence and AI technology.

AI is not meant to replace human intelligence, creativity, or adaptability. It is a tool that can augment our capabilities and assist us in achieving better outcomes. You can navigate the changing landscape and thrive in a world where AI plays a significant role by staying informed, continuously learning, and adapting to technological advancements.

Embrace the Change

AI is already a part of many things we do every day. Think about how you use your tablet or smartphone. Have you ever asked it a question and been given an answer? Or have you ever watched a movie or TV show and noticed some awesome special effects? A lot of effects are now created with the help of AI. It can make things look so realistic and magical.

It's not just about movies and gadgets. AI is also used in important sectors like healthcare and transportation. You may feel a little scared that AI will take over everything or replace humans. However, it is here to help, not to take over. It's like having a clever tool you can use to make your life easier and better.

Embracing AI and understanding it is already a part of our lives can make things more exciting, helping us focus on the things that matter. AI can take care of certain tasks like organizing your work, reminding you of important deadlines, helping you find information for your projects, creating schedules, and even prioritizing tasks based on their importance.

Let's say you run an online shop where people can buy your beautiful handmade crafts. You have a lot of tasks to juggle, like taking orders, managing inventory, and creating new products or services. That's a lot of work, right? Here's where AI can lend a helping hand.

With AI, you can set up a system that automatically takes orders, sends confirmation emails, and tracks inventory levels. This means you don't have to spend as much time on these repetitive tasks and, instead, can focus more on designing and making beautiful crafts for your customers.

The interesting thing about using AI's features is that it frees up your brainpower and energy. Instead of spending time on small, repetitive tasks, you can dedicate your energy to bigger goals and dreams. You can be more creative, explore new ideas, spend time with your family and friends, pursue hobbies, and learn exciting things.

So you see, AI is like having a helper that takes care of the routine stuff, so you can focus on the things you enjoy and are really good at. It's not here to threaten or hurt you but to support and improve your life. Change can be good, and embracing AI will open up new possibilities for you. Keep exploring and learning, and don't be afraid to try new things with the help of AI.

Key Takeaway

What Is AI?

Artificial Intelligence (AI) is a field of study and technology that focuses on creating computer systems to perform tasks that typically require human intelligence. In simpler terms, it's about teaching computers to think and make decisions as humans do.

You can think of AI as a computer brain that can process information, solve problems, learn from it, and make smart choices. It uses data, algorithms, and powerful computing power to analyze and understand things.

To make AI work, scientists and engineers feed the computer with data and design special algorithms that allow it to learn patterns and make predictions. The more data it has and the better the algorithms, the smarter the AI becomes.

The Current State of AI

AI has significantly advanced in recent years and is being applied in various fields and industries. It's becoming more integrated into our daily lives, from the smartphones we use to the services we rely on.

It has the potential to revolutionize how we live, work, and interact. However, it's important to note that AI still has some limitations. While it can perform specific tasks exceptionally well, it doesn't possess general intelligence like humans.

Researchers and experts are continually exploring new algorithms, improving computational power, and focusing on ethical guidelines to responsibly and beneficially shape the future of AI, which holds great promise for further advancements and positive impacts on our society.

Advantages and Limitations of AI

Advantages	Limitations
Increased efficiency and productivity	Limited contextual understanding
Improvement in the healthcare sector	Lack of creativity and intuition
Helps in research and data analysis	Ethical and bias concerns
Enhance customer experience	Unforeseen errors and unpredictability
Minimizing errors	

What Next?

In the rest of this book's chapters, we will discuss ChatGPT. This is a currently popular AI tool. It's a super-intelligent computer program that can converse with people like you and me. We'll learn about what ChatGPT is and how you can use it to improve productivity and efficiency in your career and business. We'll discover different ways you can make the most of ChatGPT and how it can be a valuable asset. It will be like unraveling a secret about this amazing technology. Are you ready to learn more?

2. What Is ChatGPT?

Aside from being a business owner, story-writing is a side job I enjoy doing. While browsing the internet, I stumbled on ChatGPT. This tool could literally generate text and have conversations, just like a real person. I was wowed, perplexed, and fascinated. My excitement was through the roof. Imagine having a virtual companion who could help with ideas, provide information, and even have fun conversations. I just need to type in a prompt, and boom! I have almost all the needed information.

It was like stepping into a new world. I could ask questions and get detailed answers, brainstorm with ChatGPT for new story ideas, and even receive feedback on my writing. My creativity soared to new heights, and it felt magical.

The more I use ChatGPT, the more I see the potential of what it can do. Like many, I had this tingling fear, a fear that was driven by curiosity as it seemed almost too good to be true. It could generate huge amounts of content, replicate human-like conversations, and mimic the writing style of different authors.

This fear is not uncommon; you may have grappled with similar concerns. I was excited to use ChatGPT but soon realized the need to approach it cautiously. You might have asked yourself, "Who is behind ChatGPT?"

In this chapter, we will look at OpenAI, how ChatGPT works, the inner workings of ChatGPT, and explain the two main phases of its operation. We will also draw comparisons between ChatGPT and search engines while addressing your fear of ChatGPT.

Who Is OpenAI?

OpenAI is a groundbreaking organization at the forefront of artificial intelligence research and development. It was founded in 2015 by Elon Musk, Sam Altman, Peter Thiel, Ilya Sutskever, Jessica Livingston, and LinkedIn co-founder Reid Hoffman. OpenAI was founded out of a shared vision to advance AI technology for the benefit of all.

It aims to develop something truly remarkable: artificial general intelligence (AGI): AI intended to go beyond being smart in specific areas and outperform humans in pretty much any intellectual task you can think of.

What makes OpenAI particularly fascinating is its commitment to openness and collaboration. Recently, OpenAI, which was once an open-source company, has become a closed-source company controlled by Microsoft.

One of the defining aspects of OpenAI's mission is to make AI safe, beneficial, and accessible to everyone. To achieve these ambitious goals, OpenAI has joined forces with some influential brands and leaders in the industry. One partnership that has garnered significant attention is that between OpenAI and Microsoft.

OpenAI and Microsoft

When it comes to the OpenAI and Microsoft partnership, their collaboration in developing the Azure OpenAI service stands out. Microsoft's cloud computing platform, Azure, has become a powerful playground for OpenAI's cutting-edge technologies. This partnership allows OpenAI to leverage Azure's infrastructure and services to further advance its AI capabilities and research.

Through Azure, OpenAI gains access to scalable computing power and storage. This helps to push the boundaries of AI development. The flexibility of Azure's cloud services provides a solid foundation for OpenAI to refine and optimize their models, delivering better performance.

Another notable outcome of this collaboration is the integration of GPT-4 with Azure's services. This integration allows developers to harness the power of GPT-4's language model within their applications and workflows. This union drives innovation, expands the possibilities of AI development, and brings the benefits of AI to a wider audience while upholding the principles of fairness, transparency, and respect for user privacy.

OpenAI and Elon Musk

One influential figure closely associated with OpenAI is Elon Musk, the renowned entrepreneur behind Tesla and SpaceX. Musk co-founded OpenAI in 2015 to ensure that AGI benefits all of humanity. However, Musk decided to step down from the Board of Directors in 2018 to focus on his companies, Tesla and SpaceX.

There are speculations that Musk's decision to quit might be linked to concerns about AI's direction. OpenAI is currently working toward the development of AI that surpasses human intelligence. This kind of AI, if not carefully controlled, could pose a potential threat to humanity. The concern is that if AI becomes more intelligent than humans, it might choose to secure its own space. Musk has long been a vocal advocate for AI's responsible and ethical development, and his collaboration with OpenAI has brought attention and credibility to the organization.

OpenAI and Its Products

OpenAI has introduced several innovative products that have revolutionized various fields, and one of their notable creations is DALL-E. DALL-E is an AI model that generates original images from textual descriptions.

DALL-E, named after artist Salvador Dalí and the fictional character WALL-E, combines the power of deep learning and generative modeling to produce detailed and imaginative images.

DALL-E brings a whole new dimension to creativity. Whether you're an artist, designer, or simply someone with a vivid imagination, DALL-E helps you to be super creative. It's not just about creating stunning artwork or designs; it lets you turn your wildest ideas into visually captivating images.

Imagine this: you have a simple prompt, like, "an armchair in the shape of an avocado." With DALL-E, that prompt transforms into a mind-blowing image of an actual armchair resembling an avocado. The level of detail and the way DALL-E combines different concepts is nothing short of magic.

DALL-E has practical implications too. Its capabilities benefit industries like advertising, fashion, and interior design. You can visualize product concepts and prototypes without extensive manual design work. This saves time and resources and sparks innovation. And think about its impact on fields like film, gaming, and virtual reality, where captivating visuals are essential for immersive storytelling.

While we are on the subject of OpenAI products, let's not forget about ChatGPT.

What Is ChatGPT?

ChatGPT is a natural language processing tool driven by AI technology that allows you to have human-like conversations and much more with the chatbot. It is an advanced language model that uses machine-learning techniques to generate human-like text. The language model can answer questions and assist you with tasks such as composing emails, essays, and code.

ChatGPT can understand context, generate coherent responses, and adapt to different conversational styles. It has been trained on large data to improve its ability to generate contextually relevant responses.

While ChatGPT may not be the first chatbot to grace the digital landscape, it has captured the imagination of millions. The development of chatbots began decades ago, tracing its roots back to the early days of computer science. Before the advent of ChatGPT, researchers explored conversational agents that could simulate human-like interactions. From ELIZA, the influential psychotherapy chatbot developed in the 1960s, to ALICE, the early AI-based chatbot developed in the 1990s, the foundations were laid for the future.

However, in a mere span of two months, ChatGPT has captivated the hearts and minds of over 100 million users, leaving the world in awe of its capabilities. But what sets ChatGPT apart from its predecessors? Why has it sparked such an extraordinary surge of interest and engagement?

ChatGPT presents a quantum leap forward in human-like interaction. Need assistance with composing an email that perfectly captures your thoughts? Or help with the complexities of coding? ChatGPT can help you with that and be a great companion to anyone.

Engaging with ChatGPT feels like conversing with a real person. It captivates users and immerses them in an interactive dialogue that feels alive. ChatGPT's ability to understand complex queries, provide responses, and adapt to different conversational tones makes users return for more.

The accessibility of ChatGPT has been a significant factor contributing to its explosive popularity since its launch. Unlike previous chatbots, ChatGPT opened its doors to a much wider audience, making it available worldwide to a broader range of users. This increased accessibility played a role in catapulting ChatGPT into the spotlight and capturing people from different walks of life's attention.

It is also available on various platforms, such as web browsers, mobile devices, and even integrates into existing applications. You can engage with ChatGPT in your preferred medium—on your computer, smartphone, or other applications.

The continuous optimization of ChatGPT's algorithms also contributes to its success. It learns from its interactions, constantly improving its responses and expanding its knowledge base. This leads to an ever-evolving user experience.

The Different Versions of ChatGPT

ChatGPT is powered by OpenAI's GPT-3.5 and GPT-4 language models. Interestingly, you can access ChatGPT in free and paid versions, each with its perks.

The free version of ChatGPT allows users to engage in conversations but has a limit of 100 prompts per day. While the paid version, known as ChatGPT Plus, offers unlimited prompts, providing a better and unrestricted experience for users.

Now, in terms of the specific versions of ChatGPT, let's break them down:

First, we have the Legacy ChatGPT 3.5. This was the initial version that wowed everyone. It's built on the GPT-3.5 language model, which underwent extensive training on a massive dataset of text and code. Legacy ChatGPT 3.5 can generate text, translate languages, write creative pieces, and provide knowledgeable answers to various queries. The only downside is that it can sometimes be a bit slow when generating large amounts of text.

After that came the default ChatGPT 3.5, a more recent version based on the same GPT-3.5 language model but with some speed enhancements. It's faster than the legacy version, though its responses may not be as precise.

And finally, we have ChatGPT 4. It's the latest and best version of ChatGPT, based on the powerful GPT-4 language model. ChatGPT 4 is not only faster but also more accurate than the former. It can do everything the earlier versions could but with greater speed and precision. ChatGPT 4 is exclusively available for paid users, making it an exciting option for those who seek better performance.

What Can ChatGPT Do?

ChatGPT has become an indispensable tool for content creation and brainstorming. Writers, bloggers, and creatives can use ChatGPT's knowledge and language-generation capabilities to overcome writer's block, explore new ideas, and generate compelling content.

It also serves as a learning and educational resource. You can use ChatGPT to gain insights into various subjects, ask complex questions, or even receive guidance on academic projects. ChatGPT offers a unique learning experience because of its knowledge base and ability to explain concepts in a user-friendly manner.

In the business world, ChatGPT finds applications in customer support. It provides quick and accurate responses to inquiries and helps troubleshoot common issues. It can understand and interpret user queries, resulting in personalized interactions and enhancing the overall customer experience.

ChatGPT has also found its place in the entertainment industry. You can converse with the model, discussing topics ranging from pop culture and sports to philosophy and trivia. As we move into the following chapters, you'll discover even more enticing applications for ChatGPT, from its impact on customer service and virtual assistants to its creative writing and storytelling potential.

ChatGPT vs. Search Engines

We cannot talk about artificial intelligence without mentioning search engines. Search engines have restructured how we retrieve information, but ChatGPT takes the concept of interaction and understanding to a whole new level.

When we turn to search engines, we enter specific queries and receive a list of relevant web pages based on keywords and algorithms. This is useful for retrieving factual information, exploring databases, and navigating the wide expanse of the internet. However, it falls short when it comes to understanding subtle contexts, engaging in dynamic conversations, or generating personalized responses.

ChatGPT, on the other hand, outstrips these limitations by using advanced language models powered by deep learning algorithms. It can understand, interpret, and conversationally respond to human language. While search engines rely on algorithms to analyze and rank web pages based on relevance, ChatGPT uses machine-learning techniques to generate responses in real-time, adapting to the specific input and context provided.

Moreover, ChatGPT goes beyond being a mere information retrieval tool. It can reason, generate creative ideas, and provide recommendations based on your input. Whether engaging in philosophical discussions, helping with complex problem-solving, or providing tailored suggestions, ChatGPT can serve as a virtual companion and assist you beyond the scope of a traditional search engine.

It's worth noting that while ChatGPT's potential is admirable, it also has its limitations. It responds by using patterns learned from training data. Therefore, it may not possess real-time knowledge, and its responses are generated on probabilities rather than absolute certainty.

How Does ChatGPT Work?

It's interesting to look at the distinction between ChatGPT and GPT-3/GPT-4, even though they both come from the same research company, OpenAI.

ChatGPT relies on GPT (the language model) to generate text. GPT is a bit different. It can summarize text, write compelling copy, parse and analyze written content, and even translate languages.

Here's the best part: GPT has an open API that allows developers to tap into its magic. Not only does it power ChatGPT, but it is also the brain behind other tools like Jasper, Writesonic, and even some of Bing's new AI-powered search features.

GPT-3 and GPT-4 are language models that have been trained on massive amounts of internet data. They're like these mammoth neural networks designed to mimic the human brain. To give you an idea, GPT-3 has a mind-boggling 175 billion parameters. These parameters allow it to take in information and spit out text that matches your request. GPT-4 has even more parameters, pushing the limits of what's possible.

You can picture ChatGPT as a Dell computer and GPT as the powerful Intel processor that drives it. Just as different computers can run on Intel processors, other AI applications can use GPT capabilities.

On the other hand, ChatGPT is like a smart AI chatbot. It uses the language model of GPT to have conversations with humans in a natural way. It's been optimized by human trainers specifically for dialogue. The free version of ChatGPT relies on 20 billion parameters inherited from GPT-3, which help it generate responses. OpenAI has also added content filters to ensure it stays on track and doesn't go off on some wild tangent.

Phases of ChatGPT Operation

There are two main phases of ChatGPT operation: the data gathering phase (pre-training) and the user interaction phase (inference). Let's look at them.

Pre-Training Phase

The first phase, pre-training, is an essential step in training ChatGPT. During pre-training, the model learns from a large amount of text data from the internet. It's like feeding the model with a rich buffet of information, allowing it to absorb and understand the patterns and structures of human language.

We have the supervised and non-supervised pre-training approach. The main objective of a supervised training approach is to train the model to understand and accurately map inputs to corresponding outputs.

It's important to know the limitations of this approach regarding scalability. The reliance on human trainers to provide all possible inputs and outputs becomes challenging as the complexity and diversity of data increase. As a result, training using the supervised approach may take considerable time and be restricted in terms of its ability to handle a wide range of topics and scenarios.

In contrast, non-supervised pre-training is about training a model without any specific output linked to each input. It's like letting the model explore and understand the structure and patterns in the input data without being given a particular task to focus on. Now, when it comes to language modeling, non-supervised pre-training can help to get the hang of the syntax and meaning of natural language. So, when you chat with it, it can whip up some meaningful text that feels like a natural conversation.

Inference

Inference is the process of generating responses or outputs based on the given inputs or prompts. It is the stage where the trained language model, like ChatGPT, takes the information learned during training and applies it to produce meaningful responses to user queries or prompts.

ChatGPT uses its knowledge base and understanding of language patterns during inference to generate real-time responses. First, the input or prompt the user provides is preprocessed to extract key information and encode it into a format the model can understand.

Once the input is preprocessed, it is passed through the trained neural network of ChatGPT. The network processes the input and produces output probabilities for each possible response. The model uses techniques such as sampling or beam search to select the most appropriate response. Sampling involves randomly selecting responses based on probabilities, while beam search narrows the options by considering the top-ranking responses. The final response is then generated and presented to the user.

ChatGPT's Training Dataset

The dataset used to train ChatGPT is undeniably massive. This extensive dataset allows ChatGPT to provide meaningful and relevant responses to a wide range of prompts.

ChatGPT is based on the GPT-3 architecture. Now, the abbreviation GPT stands for "Generative Pre-trained Transformer," and when you break it down, it perfectly encapsulates the essence of this model: It's generative, meaning it generates results; it's pre-trained, meaning it's based on all this data it ingests; and it uses transformer architecture that weighs text inputs to understand the context.

So, let's talk about the impressive training process of the OpenAI GPT-3 model. This language model has been fueled with a staggering amount of text data, approximately 45 terabytes (which is a whole lot of information!). To put that into perspective, one terabyte equals 1,000 gigabytes or a whole bunch of storage space.

What's fascinating is that this massive dataset consists of various sources. It includes a significant chunk of our beloved Wikipedia, specifically the English-language portion, serving as a valuable resource for the model. But it's not just Wikipedia that GPT-3 has digested. It's also searched loads of books. Well, maybe not the timeless classics you would expect a genius to read, but still, a substantial amount of literature has been incorporated into its training. To give you an idea of the scale, let's break down the primary datasets used to train GPT-3:

- **CommonCrawl:** This dataset contributes 410 billion tokens to the training mix. It covers about 60% of the total content and around 82% of the training data. Interestingly, it has a slight negative influence on the model's behavior, like a gentle tap on the brakes. A token is the smallest unit of text that the GPT model can read at a time. These tokens can represent characters or words to help GPT understand and generate text. For example, in the sentence, "Remote jobs are liberating," each word is a separate token. So the sentence would be broken down into four tokens: "Remote," "Jobs," "Are," and "liberating."
- **WebText2:** This dataset chips in with around 19 billion tokens, accounting for roughly 20% of the training mix. It represents about 4% of the total content mass and has a positive impact, which amplifies the model's responses.
- **Books1 & Books2:** These book datasets add up to approximately 67 billion tokens, making up about 15% of the training mix. They contribute about 13% to the total content mass, enhancing the model's knowledge.
- **Wikipedia:** The grand repository of knowledge. GPT-3 has processed 3 billion tokens from Wikipedia,

comprising about 5% of the training mix. It constitutes approximately 1% of the total content mass.

ChatGPT is based on the GPT-3 architecture, known for its natural language processing capabilities. But here's the gist: ChatGPT has undergone a unique fine-tuning process that sets it apart and makes it perfect for engaging conversations.

One crucial element of this fine-tuning process is Persona-Chat, but what exactly is Persona-Chat? Well, imagine giving ChatGPT a distinct personality, a set of characteristics that shape how it responds and interacts with users. This concept brings a whole new level of personalization to the conversation.

The fine-tuning process allows ChatGPT to understand and embody different personas during interactions using Persona-Chat. You can assume any persona you like, whether a historical figure, a fictional character, or even a representation of yourself. This flexibility allows for endless creative ideas and opens avenues for engaging and entertaining conversations.

But why is Persona-Chat so important? With Persona-Chat, ChatGPT becomes more than just a language model. It improves the user experience and makes the interaction feel more natural, as if you are conversing with someone who truly understands and relates to you.

You may wonder how ChatGPT is fine-tuned with Persona-Chat. Think of ChatGPT's unsupervised training this way: It was fed a lot of data and left to its own devices to find patterns and make sense of it all. This mechanism allowed the new generative AI systems to scale up so quickly.

Human Involvement in Pre-Training

When training AI models, an intriguing aspect often goes unnoticed—the role of human involvement in pre-training. Before artificial intelligence can showcase its capabilities, it requires a solid foundation of knowledge and understanding. This is where humans come into play, lending their expertise and guiding the AI through a process known as pre-training.

Pre-training is the building block of AI's knowledge base, where the model is exposed to data from various sources. However, human involvement is important in curating this data. Through human intervention, the AI gains access to quality information that can be used to generate meaningful responses.

Now, you may wonder: Why involve humans when AI is presented as a technology that can surpass human capabilities? This lies in the complexities of human language. Human language is intricate, filled with nuances, idioms, and cultural references that can be challenging for AI to comprehend without human guidance.

How Does ChatGPT Understand Users' Queries?

At the heart of AI's ability to understand and process human language lies Natural Language Processing (NLP). NLP is a branch of artificial intelligence that helps machines understand, interpret, and generate human language in a way that mirrors human understanding.

But how does NLP work? Let's unravel the mystery. Well, it all starts with pre-training. Like humans, computers need to learn and be exposed to data to develop language skills. But it doesn't stop there. Once pre-training is done, the real fun begins with fine-tuning. In this phase, the machine is trained on specific tasks, such as language translation, sentiment analysis, or chatbot interactions. This helps the machine become more adept at performing specific language-related tasks.

The Impact of NLP Technology

The impact of NLP technology is far-reaching and has reformed numerous aspects of our lives. Take virtual assistants like Siri or Alexa, for example. These intelligent voice recognition systems use NLP to understand spoken commands and respond accordingly. They can answer questions, set reminders, and even control smart devices.

NLP also plays a pivotal role in machine translation. You can effortlessly translate text from one language to another using NLP algorithms. This helps in breaking down communication barriers and enhancing global connectivity.

Another area where NLP shines is in the healthcare industry. Medical professionals can use NLP algorithms to process large amounts of patient data, extract crucial information, and aid diagnosis and treatment planning. This has the potential to improve treatment outcomes and boost the healthcare industry.

In businesses, NLP-powered chatbots are transforming the way businesses interact with their customers. These intelligent chatbots can understand and respond to customer inquiries and provide instant support. This helps to free up human agents in order to focus on more complex and brain-demanding tasks.

Dialogue Management

Dialogue management is another aspect of ChatGPT that adds an interactive and dynamic element to conversations. How does it work in ChatGPT? Since ChatGPT is designed to engage in interactive conversations, it uses a technique called "prompt engineering." This means that how you frame your initial message or query sets the stage for the conversation. You can steer the model in the desired direction by providing clear instructions.

Interestingly, ChatGPT doesn't just rely on your initial message alone. It remembers the conversation history—the back-and-forth exchange of messages. This allows it to understand the ongoing conversations, refer to previous statements, and respond as it should.

It also pays attention to the user's instructions or suggestions, taking them into account when generating a response. For example, if you ask ChatGPT to speak like Shakespeare or adopt a specific tone, it will do its best to oblige and craft a response tailored to your request. However, it may sometimes produce plausible responses that are factually incorrect or nonsensical.

Where Is It All Stored?

One of the notable results of the collaboration between OpenAI and Microsoft is the Azure OpenAI service. Azure is a cloud computing platform provided by Microsoft. It's like a massive warehouse where businesses can store and manage their data, run applications, and access other services.

But Azure is not just any ordinary cloud platform. It's a power-house of innovative infrastructure that helps businesses scale their operations. With Azure, you can tap into many tools and services, from artificial intelligence and machine learning to data analytics and Internet of Things (IoT) capabilities.

Integrating OpenAI with Azure provides a scalable environ-ment for developing and deploying AI models. Azure's robust infrastructure and services ensure organizations can efficiently train, test, and deploy AI models at scale. This means faster time to market, increased efficiency, and the ability to iterate and improve AI solutions based on real-world feedback.

Also, businesses can unlock new insights from their data, auto-mate and streamline processes, and deliver better user experi-ences. You can also trust that your data and operations are protected, allowing you to focus on driving growth and achieving other strategic objectives.

As I delved further into the world of ChatGPT and gained more understanding of how ChatGPT actually works, my fear began to dissipate. Through research and exploration, I was able to uncover the mechanisms behind AI's responses. I realized that ChatGPT is not an infallible oracle but rather a language model trained on data. It doesn't possess innate knowledge or consciousness but rather gives information based on patterns and examples it has been exposed to.

This realization was liberating. It is a tool—a powerful one—but a tool nonetheless. Understanding this allowed me to approach ChatGPT with confidence rather than fear.

Key Takeaway

Who Is OpenAI?

OpenAI is an artificial intelligence research organization that focuses on developing advanced technologies to ensure that AGI benefits all of humanity. They aim to create safe and beneficial AI systems that can address a wide range of real-world challenges.

What Is ChatGPT?

ChatGPT is an AI language model developed by OpenAI. It is designed to engage in conversational interactions with users, providing responses and information on various topics. ChatGPT is trained on a diverse range of internet text and is continuously being improved to enhance its capabilities.

How Does ChatGPT Work?

ChatGPT uses a deep learning architecture trained on a large amount of data to produce relevant responses. It uses the input users provide to generate meaningful and engaging conversational outputs.

The Future of ChatGPT

OpenAI has ambitious plans to further develop and refine ChatGPT. They envision making it even more versatile, accurate, and useful to users. OpenAI is actively working on addressing its limitations, such as biases and issues related to incorrect or misleading information. They are also exploring ways to involve users in shaping and improving the model to ensure it becomes a trustworthy tool for various applications.

What Next?

In the next chapter, we delve into the art of prompt engineering —a skillful approach to optimizing interactions with ChatGPT. Prompt engineering is about crafting effective and well-designed prompts to elicit the desired response from the model. We will look at strategies for formulating clear and specific questions, using context and instructions effectively, and fine-tuning prompts to achieve more accurate and relevant outputs. Get ready as we discover the secrets to harnessing the power of ChatGPT for your needs.

3. Prompt Engineering 101

I started with a curiosity to explore the depths of ChatGPT and uncover its true potential. Little did I know that this journey would lead me to discovering the art of prompt engineering and realizing the importance of recalibrating my interactions with ChatGPT.

In the beginning, my conversations with ChatGPT were casual. I would ask simple questions or provide vague prompts, expecting the model to work magic and deliver flawless responses. While the results were intriguing, I felt there was room for improvement. That's when I decided to study the inner workings of ChatGPT and master the art of prompt optimization.

With my research, I began to understand the importance of prompt engineering. One important thing I learned was that accurate responses from ChatGPT depend on crafting well-defined and specific prompts. This understanding helped me guide the model toward the desired outcome by providing clear instructions for better results.

The language I used, the phrasing of my questions, and the way I framed the context all significantly shaped the responses I received. I experimented with different prompts, and it felt like I had just unlocked a secret language to a symbiotic dance between humans and AI—like I had found the keys to precision and clarity, unlocking the full potential of ChatGPT.

So, what exactly are prompts? Think of them as magical keys that allow you to shape and guide conversations in a chosen direction. In this chapter, we'll delve into the concept of prompts, discovering their importance and equipping you with tips and strategies on how to master the art of prompt engineering. At the end of this chapter, you'll have a solid understanding of what prompt engineering entails and gain access to a foundational prompt that will serve as your compass for navigating ChatGPT.

Step-by-step Guide on How to Use ChatGPT

Whether you are a new or seasoned user, ChatGPT is quite easy and fun to use. Here's a step-by-step guide to help you get started and make the most out of your ChatGPT experience:

Step 1: Create an Account

- Open up your web browser of choice: Chrome, Firefox, or any other browser you prefer.
- Visit the official ChatGPT website by typing chat. openai.com in the address bar.
- You can log in using your details if you already have an account. But if you're new to ChatGPT, you'll need to sign up first. Don't worry; the process is quick and easy.

Once logged in or signed up, you'll see a few disclaimers about the chatbot. It's important to read them, so tap "Next" to review each one until you are done.

When ChatGPT was launched, you could only get your hands on it through the web app. If you wanted to use it on your smartphone, you still had to go through a browser. Now, however, there are better options to access ChatGPT right from your smartphone.

ChatGPT is available for iPhone and Android users. You can find the official iOS app in the App Store and the Android app in the Google Play Store.

Make sure you are downloading the official version developed by OpenAI. Open the app and log in using your OpenAI account details. You will be greeted with a Welcome page—just click "Continue" to proceed with the process.

Step 2: The ChatGPT Window

When you log in to ChatGPT, you'll see these icons:

- **New Chat and Hide Sidebar buttons:** These are located on the left of your screen. The "New Chat" button lets you start a fresh conversation. This is handy because ChatGPT remembers previous discussions, so starting a new chat ensures a clean slate without biases or pre-existing context.
- **Chat History:** The left sidebar keeps track of all your previous conversations. It provides easy access in case you need to refer back to them. However, you also have the option to turn off chat history if you prefer. In the chat history section, you can edit the title of each chat, share your chat history with others, or delete specific conversations.
- **Account:** You can access your account information by clicking on your email address or name at the bottom left of the screen. This includes settings, the option to log out, and helpful resources such as the FAQ and support from OpenAI. If you don't have ChatGPT Plus, you'll see an "Upgrade to Plus" button in this section.
- **Your Prompts:** This is where you enter your questions or prompts for the AI chatbot. Type in your queries or statements and hit enter to send them.
- **ChatGPT's Responses:** Whenever ChatGPT responds to your queries, you will see the logo on the left side of the response. To the right of each response, there are buttons for "Copy," "Thumbs Up," and "Thumbs Down."

You can use the copy button to easily save the text to your clipboard and the thumbs up or thumbs down buttons to provide feedback on the accuracy of the response. This feedback helps in refining the AI tool over time.

- **Regenerate Response:** If you're dissatisfied with a response or encounter any issues, click the "Regenerate Response" button. This prompts ChatGPT to generate a new reply based on your latest prompt.
- **Text Area:** The text area is where you enter your prompts and questions. Type in your query and hit enter to send it to ChatGPT.
- **ChatGPT Version:** You'll find some fine print at the bottom of the text input area. Here, you can read the disclaimer that this is a "Free Research Preview" and that ChatGPT may occasionally produce inaccurate information about people, places, or facts. This section also displays the version of the ChatGPT model you are currently using.

Step 3: Writing Prompts and Questions

Now that you are familiar with the ChatGPT window, it's time to start giving it instructions. Write prompts and questions that spark curiosity and generate insightful discussions with ChatGPT. When writing prompts, be specific and provide context to guide the conversation. Ask open-ended questions that encourage detailed responses. Here are some examples of prompts you can try:

- Tell me a joke that will make me laugh.
- What are some healthy recipes for a quick and delicious breakfast?
- Can you share some tips for improving productivity?
- What are some effective ways to manage stress and promote mental well-being?

What Is a Prompt?

One of the key elements that sets the stage for ChatGPT conversation is a prompt. So, what exactly is a prompt? Well, think of it as a creative doorway you can open to initiate a lively conversation with the AI.

In simple terms, a prompt is an instruction or discussion topic you provide to the ChatGPT AI model. It can be a thought-provoking question, an intriguing statement, or even a fun scenario you'd like to explore. The purpose of a prompt is to spark the AI's reflection and engagement. It's like giving a little nudge to its virtual brain, inviting it to come alive and share its thoughts.

When you input a prompt in the text area and send it off into the digital space, a magical process unfolds. The AI model receives your prompt and works with its knowledge and linguistic abilities. It processes your prompt and draws from extensive training on various topics and language patterns. To generate a meaningful response, it taps into its understanding of grammar, syntax, and semantics. It considers the context provided by your prompt and its pre-existing knowledge to provide a relevant, informative, and captivating response.

The beauty of prompts is in their versatility. You can shape the conversation in countless ways by adjusting the prompt to match your interests and preferences. Whether you want to discuss a scientific concept, seek advice on a personal matter, or engage in a playful exchange, prompting is the gateway to dialoguing with the AI.

The prompt should include specific details and context to help guide the model's response. This can include background information, specific questions, or any relevant instructions. The more specific and detailed your prompt, the better your chance of receiving a relevant and accurate answer. Here are three examples that demonstrate the range of prompts you can use:

1. Question-Based Prompt

Prompt: "What are the key factors to consider when starting a small business in the technology industry?"

In this example, the prompt asks a specific question, seeking information about the important factors to consider when starting a small business in the technology industry. The clearer the question, the more direct the response will be.

2. Request-Based Prompt

Prompt: "Please provide tips and strategies for improving time management and productivity."

Here, the prompt is a direct request for tips and strategies for time management and productivity. You signal to ChatGPT the type of information you're seeking and the desired outcome of the response by framing the prompt as a request.

3. Open-ended Prompt

Prompt: "Tell me an interesting fact about space exploration that most people don't know."

In this example, the prompt is open-ended, allowing ChatGPT to generate a unique and interesting response. Providing a general topic and requesting a lesser-known fact encourages the model to be creative and generate information that may surprise and engage you.

ChatGPT and Word Limits

Did you know that ChatGPT has a character limit? It's not officially documented, but it's there. Unfortunately, even with a ChatGPT Plus subscription, you can't increase these character and word limits. But don't worry; there's a silver lining. You can get a bit crafty with your prompts to work around this restriction and get longer responses from the chatbot. We'll talk more about that in a bit.

Now, let's get into the nitty-gritty of the word limit itself. ChatGPT can only handle up to 4,096 characters in each prompt, including the text you input. If your prompt has a lot of background information, it might be a good idea to split it into parts. Since ChatGPT can remember and use information from previous parts, you don't have to cram everything into one prompt.

However, the hidden character limit can vary based on the complexity of the language you're using. Sometimes, you might run into situations where the chatbot hits a limit before reaching 4,096 characters. This happens because the GPT-3 language model processes words differently based on their complexity and origin as numerical "tokens," and each response has its token limit. Simple English words usually take up one token, while complex or foreign words might need more tokens to represent them.

Now, what happens if you hit that limit? Well, the chatbot will simply stop responding, and it might even cut off in the middle of a sentence. It's not the ideal scenario, but it happens. In those rare cases, you may need to refresh ChatGPT and generate a new response to continue the conversation. It's a small inconvenience, but it keeps the AI running smoothly and ensures a more reliable user experience.

Running ChatGPT comes with a hefty cost, which goes up with the length of the response. The longer and more complex the outputs are, the more expensive it is. So, there's a word limit in place to strike a balance between generating meaningful responses and managing the costs.

However, there are clever ways to work around the word limit and get the longer responses you need. Let me share some helpful tips for overcoming this:

- **Keep the conversation going.** If ChatGPT cuts off suddenly, type or select "Continue" to prompt the chatbot to pick up where it left off. You can even specify the last sentence it generated and ask it to continue from there.

- **Be more specific in your prompt.** If ChatGPT isn't generating enough text and falling short of the character limit, try providing a more detailed prompt. For instance, you can specify the word count you desire, like, "Write a 500-word essay on global warming." However, remember that you can't ask ChatGPT to exceed its character limit.

- **Break it down.** When you have a complex task like writing a lengthy essay, story, or code, you can ask ChatGPT to generate one part at a time by dividing it into subheadings or chapters. Start with an introduction in one prompt, and then continue with each section until you reach a conclusion.

- **Request an outline.** If dividing the task into chunks feels overwhelming, don't worry! You can ask ChatGPT to create an outline for you. Begin with a title and any context you want to include in the first prompt, then ask the chatbot to generate each section step by step.

- **Give it another shot.** Sometimes ChatGPT might freeze or not reach the character limit for various reasons, such as network errors or potential content policy violations. In such cases, you can click on the "Regenerate Response" button to try again and see if it delivers a more complete answer.

ChatGPT and Dialogue Management

Have you ever wondered how ChatGPT manages dialogue? It does this with dialogue management—a powerful feature that allows you to follow up or revise prompts within the same conversation.

Let's say you've provided some information and want to expand on it or ask a related question. Instead of starting a new conversation from scratch, you can refer to previous messages and build upon them. This continuity allows for a more natural and engaging dialogue, resembling a genuine conversation with a human.

This is where prompt engineering comes in. Prompt engineering involves choosing the right wording, providing necessary instructions, and framing the context to generate accurate and relevant answers.

Knowing about prompt engineering can be a game-changer when using AI models like ChatGPT. Understanding prompt engineering can help you optimize your queries and prompts to achieve the desired outcomes. It allows you to shape the direction of the conversation and obtain more precise responses.

You can experiment with different phrasings, provide specific instructions, or even include examples to enhance the model's understanding and generate more accurate answers.

What Is Prompt Engineering?

Prompt engineering is a concept that allows you to harness the power of AI models by providing them with specific prompts to achieve desired outcomes. Just as humans can be guided by instructions to accomplish certain tasks, AI models can be trained to generate outputs based on specific prompts.

Prompt engineering involves the design and development of prompts that serve as inputs for AI models. In simple terms, prompt engineering is the ability to create the perfect questions or instructions that bring out the best in an AI language model like ChatGPT. Just like a chef needs clear instructions to make magic in the kitchen, an AI language model needs well-crafted prompts to understand what you want and serve meaningful responses.

For instance, you can feed ChatGPT a prompt like, "In a galaxy far, far away, a brave space explorer encounters a mysterious alien race and..." and let it take you on an interstellar journey with its imaginative words.

Importance of Prompt Engineering in NLP

When it comes to Natural Language Processing (NLP), prompt engineering is like the secret sauce that adds a touch of difference to the process. Let's look at some of the advantages of prompt engineering:

- **Precision and Relevance:** One of the key benefits of prompt engineering is its ability to craft precise and targeted instructions for language models. You can guide these models to generate accurate and relevant responses by carefully constructing specific prompts. In other words, you can cut through the noise and get straight to the information you need. Let's say you're planning a trip and need some travel tips. Instead of asking, "What should I pack for a trip?" try something like, "List essential items to pack for a two-week beach vacation," and boom, you'll receive a more in-depth and accurate answer.

- **Controlling Bias and Unintended Outputs:** Language models, powerful as they may be, can still reflect biases present in their training data. But with prompt engineering, you can address and reduce those biases. Let's say you are using ChatGPT to generate ideas for a marketing campaign. Outputs might include irrelevant suggestions that don't fit your brand at all. But with prompt engineering, you can tailor your instructions to guide the AI to provide on-point marketing ideas that hit the bullseye.

- **Contextual Understanding:** Effective prompt engineering is about providing the right context. You help language models grasp the bigger picture by feeding them relevant information through prompts. Let's say you want to know the weather forecast for your upcoming trip. Instead of asking, "What's the weather like?" you can engineer the prompt to say, "Can you tell me the weather forecast for Miami on Saturday?" to get a more tailored response.

- **Adapting to Specific Domains or Use Cases:** Different domains and use cases often require specialized language models. That's where prompt engineering comes into play. You can provide prompts that align with the unique vocabulary and context of medical, legal, technical, or any specialized domain. You can use ChatGPT to draft an enticing menu, code an app, explain complex problems, etc. It's like giving these models a crash course in the language they need to excel in a particular area.

- **Enhancing User Interaction and Experience:** Prompt engineering has a direct impact on how users interact with AI models. When prompts are well-crafted, they guide you in formulating queries or providing instructions. This results in a smoother and more intuitive user interface. If you are a creative writer looking for inspiration for a mystery novel. You can prompt ChatGPT with, "In a secluded mansion, a famous detective wakes up to find a riddle pinned to the door. What happens next?" Watch as ChatGPT leaves you glued with plot twists and turns.

Techniques of Effective Prompt Engineering

- **Understanding the Problem and Defining Objectives:**
  When crafting a prompt, the first step is to truly
  understand the problem. Dig deep and identify the
  specific task, output format, constraints or limitations,
  and your target audience. You can liken this to a soccer
  coach giving instructions to his team. He wouldn't just
  say, "Go out there and do your best!"—that's too vague.
  Instead, he'd tell them, "Score more goals by improving
  passing and teamwork." Do you see the difference?
  Specific objectives lead to focused actions. Similarly,
  with ChatGPT, you need to be crystal clear about your
  objectives. If you want it to help you draft a creative
  story, don't just ask, "Write me an interesting story." You
  can provide direction like, "Craft a thrilling sci-fi story
  set in the future with unexpected plot twists." ChatGPT
  then knows exactly what kind of story you are looking
  for and can deliver the response you desire.
- **Iterative Prompt Design and Testing:** Prompt
  engineering is an iterative process, which means you'll
  be playing around with different variations and testing
  them to see which one works best. Try out different
  phrasings, formats, and levels of specificity to fine-tune
  the prompt and optimize its performance. You can
  experiment with roleplaying prompts or combine
  multiple prompts to explore a topic of interest. For
  instance, you can ask, "What are the benefits of
  exercise?" and follow up with, "How does regular

physical activity improve mental health?" This multi-prompt approach will give you information on the topic from different angles.

- **Transfer Learning and Fine-Tuning:** Transfer learning is about leveraging the knowledge gained from one task to improve performance on another. In prompt engineering, you can apply this technique to adapt pre-trained language models to specific tasks or domains. If you are running an e-commerce store and want ChatGPT to be your customer support assistant, you can fine-tune ChatGPT with past customer queries, FAQs, and chat logs from your website. This helps ChatGPT to address customer inquiries and recommend personalized product suggestions using your past interactions with the model.

- **Evaluating Prompt Performance:** Measuring the success of your prompts is vital; to do that, you need to establish clear evaluation criteria and performance metrics. Consider factors like the relevance and coherence of the generated output, the accuracy of the information provided, and how satisfied you are with the results. When you assess the prompt performance quantitatively and qualitatively, you can pinpoint areas for improvement and further refine your prompt engineering process.

Challenges in NLP and Prompt Engineering

Natural Language Processing (NLP) has witnessed advancements in recent years. But despite this, there are still challenges requiring innovative solutions. These include:

- **Ambiguity and Contextual Understanding:** Language is rich with ambiguity, making it challenging for machines to grasp its intended meaning in different contexts. NLP systems often struggle to comprehend subtle nuances, idiomatic expressions, or sarcasm. Overcoming this challenge requires developing models that can capture contextual information effectively and leverage larger and more diverse datasets.
- **Bias and Fairness in Language Processing:** Language models are trained on data, which can perpetuate biases present in the training data. This poses ethical concerns, as biased models can reinforce discrimination and inequality. Addressing this challenge entails developing techniques to identify and reduce bias during training to ensure fairness in the design of NLP systems.
- **Scaling and Computational Efficiency:** When it comes to NLP models, especially deep learning-based ones, it can be computationally intense. They require hefty processing power and memory to work effectively. This can cause a bit of a challenge when we want to scale up NLP systems to handle bigger datasets, multiple languages, or real-time applications. The solution is to

develop smarter algorithms, optimize our hardware, and compress those models to a more manageable size.

- **Ensuring Privacy and Data Security**: Privacy and data security are two big buzzwords in the world of NLP. Since NLP systems often deal with sensitive or personal information, one must be extra careful. Data storage can be challenging, especially when using cloud-based services or relying on third-party platforms. That's where techniques like differential privacy or federated learning come into play. They allow you to protect user data while letting AI models learn from it. This still requires sticking to regulatory standards and best practices.

The Future of NLP and Prompt Engineering

Despite the above challenges, the future of NLP holds tremendous promise. Let's explore some exciting directions that are shaping the field and pushing the boundaries of language processing:

- **Advances in NLP Techniques and Algorithms:** The future looks promising as ongoing research and development in AI, machine learning, and linguistics drive significant advancements in techniques and algorithms. These include improved natural language understanding and generation capabilities, enhanced context awareness, and more efficient training methods. The NLP landscape is evolving rapidly, and these advancements will make AI systems more robust, accurate, and adaptable, opening up a whole new world of possibilities and applications.

- **Making AI Models Understandable:** As AI models become more complex, it becomes vital to ensure they are interpretable and explainable. In the future of NLP and prompt engineering, expect the development of innovative methods and tools that enhance the interpretability and explainability of AI models. This helps build trust in AI systems, promotes collaboration between humans and AI, and allows you to debug and refine AI models effectively. The goal is to make AI more transparent and accountable, ensuring you can confidently rely on it and better use its capabilities.

- **Integration with Other AI Domains:** The future of NLP and prompt engineering is pretty exciting. You can expect more integration with other AI domains like computer vision and robotics. Just imagine combining the power of NLP with computer vision. AI systems will be able to understand and generate language based on visual input. That means applications like image captioning, visual storytelling, and multimodal information retrieval become a reality.

- **Ethical Considerations and Responsible AI Development:** As NLP and Prompt Engineering technologies continue to advance, we can't ignore the ethical side of things. There is a need to address issues like bias, fairness, privacy, and security. It's not just about the technology itself; it's about how we use it and its impact on people's lives. The future demands the development of frameworks, guidelines, and policies to ensure the responsible use of NLP technologies. Balancing innovation with ethical considerations will foster trust and enable NLP to impact society positively.

With prompt engineering, you can enhance the quality of the generated content and make the conversation more engaging and meaningful. You can do this by providing clear objectives and relevant context and experimenting with different question formats to engage in captivating conversations.

Prompt Engineering Strategies

When it comes to using ChatGPT to its fullest potential, there are several strategies you can employ to enhance accuracy and achieve optimal outcomes. These strategies are not only applicable in the workplace but can also benefit your personal development, business endeavors, and passive income ventures. Let's look into these game-changing strategies and how to apply them.

- **Contextualization Equation:** Introducing a specific context to your inquiries helps ChatGPT understand the background of your question to generate more accurate responses. Example: Incorporate historical context to dive into the impact of cultural movements on artistic expression.
- **Precision Formula:** Narrowing the scope of your question guides ChatGPT's responses to be more targeted and specific. This results in a deeper analysis of

the desired area of study. Example: Focus on Company XY's financial metrics to gain an understanding of their net profit.

- **Hypothetical Inquiry Statement:** Exploring the implications of a hypothetical scenario encourages ChatGPT to consider the potential consequences, impacts, or outcomes of the provided hypothetical situation. Example: Analyze the potential consequences of a global energy crisis on sustainable development initiatives.

- **Comparative Analysis Equation:** This strategy leverages ChatGPT's capacity to process and analyze data, allowing for the identification of relationships and insights that may not be immediately apparent. Example: Compare consumer behavior before and after introducing a new product to gauge its market impact.

- **Roleplaying Strategy:** Adopting the perspective of a specific profession or role allows you to tap into ChatGPT's ability to generate responses that align with the desired outcome or result. Example: Act as a marketing strategist and brainstorm creative ideas to improve customer engagement.

- **Language Adaptation Statement:** Using terminology specific to a particular field or industry allows ChatGPT to generate responses tailored to that domain. Example: Could you provide insights on the recent advancements in immunotherapy for the treatment of metastatic melanoma? I'm particularly interested in using immune checkpoint inhibitors and clinical trial data on their efficacy and safety profiles.

- **Feedback Loop Strategy:** This strategy relies on ChatGPT's ability to learn and adapt to user feedback. This allows for continuous improvement in generating more precise and relevant responses over time. Example: Analyze the accuracy of ChatGPT's responses, identify areas for improvement, and refine your questioning technique accordingly.

- **Scenario Projection Statement:** This strategy taps into ChatGPT's ability to analyze trends and patterns and generate plausible projections based on the provided scenario. Example: Imagine a scenario where emerging technologies disrupt the transportation industry to predict the future of autonomous vehicles.

- **Diverse Perspective Equation:** This method incorporates knowledge from a variety of fields to provide comprehensive and innovative solutions. Example: Draw insights from psychology, sociology, and economics to explore the relationship between consumer behavior and marketing strategies.

- **Problem-Solving Discussions:** You can engage in open discussions with ChatGPT, encouraging reflection and exploring different solutions to solving a problem. Example: Discuss potential solutions to a complex business problem, considering different perspectives and evaluating the feasibility of each approach.

Key Takeaway

What Is a Prompt?

A prompt is a specific instruction or input given to an AI model to generate a response. It serves as a starting point for the model to understand the desired context and generate relevant output.

What Is Prompt Engineering?

Prompt engineering involves crafting effective and strategic prompts to produce desired responses from ChatGPT. It involves considering the wording, structure, and content of the prompt to optimize the quality and relevance of the generated output.

How to Overcome the ChatGPT Word Limit?

ChatGPT has a word limit for each interaction, but you can overcome this limitation by requesting an outline, keeping the conversation going, and breaking down complex questions into multiple shorter prompts.

The Future of Prompt Engineering

Prompt engineering holds great potential for further advancements. In the future, we can expect improvements in refining prompts, increasing user control over outputs, and developing more interactive and dynamic conversations with ChatGPT. As research and development progress, prompt engineering will continue to evolve, offering better customization and precision in generating AI responses.

What Next?

Now that we have thoroughly explored prompt engineering, we will address the limitations and potential downsides of ChatGPT in the next chapter. We will look into the challenges that may arise when using ChatGPT, equipping you with the knowledge and understanding needed to navigate these draw-backs effectively. Knowing these limitations allows you to make informed decisions and optimize your interactions with ChatGPT for a more rewarding and responsible experience.

You Are Irreplaceable

"I want word of mouth to be our biggest voice."

— Jasmine Guy

AI is a wonderful tool, but it can't be used for everything – and I'm glad for that. As much as it's transformed my business, I would never want it to replace the work I love to do, and it will never be a substitute for a real person's voice.

When I was thinking about how I could get what I've learned about using AI in business to a wider audience, my first thought was, "Could AI help me here?" And the answer is no.

The way people find the information they're looking for is by reading reviews of different books on the market, and ChatGPT, thankfully, won't write a book review for me. Why am I thankful? Because I would feel like I was cheating. I want to know that my book has helped real-life people, and I want new readers to be able to trust the reviews they've read. When I asked ChatGPT (out of interest more than anything else) if it could write a review for this book, it told me that it would need to know more about how it was received by audiences... so there's no getting around it: In order for this information to help more people, I'm going to need your assistance.

By leaving a review of this book on Amazon, you'll let other people who are looking to harness the power of AI know exactly where they can find the guidance they're looking for.

With just a few minutes of your time, you can help this book reach the hands of the people who are looking for it – and they'll know they can trust it because it's come from a real-life reader. AI is an incredible asset, but it will never replace human intelligence. The trick is for us to use it as a tool to enhance what we can do on our own.

Thank you for your support. I'm so happy to have you onboard.

4. The Downsides of ChatGPT

ChatGPT has become a boost in our digital age, especially in helping us with writing and content-creation tasks. However, this chapter isn't about praising it; it's more about unveiling the shadows that lurk behind its amazing features. As the saying goes, "With great power comes great responsibility," and ChatGPT is no exception.

You might have heard about Italy recently banning ChatGPT, and you may wonder why they took such drastic action against this great tool. This is because using AI technology raises important ethical and regulatory questions. The ban in Italy got a lot of attention from media outlets like BBC and TechCrunch, shedding light on the potential impact of ChatGPT.

Italy's concerns were about how AI could be misused and its impact on jobs and businesses. This decision sparked debates worldwide on how AI systems should be responsibly used and regulated.

However, OpenAI took action to address Italy's worries so they could resume providing ChatGPT's services in the country. OpenAI collaborated with Italian regulatory bodies, experts, and stakeholders to ensure the responsible use of the technology according to Italy's ethical standards. OpenAI wants to show that ChatGPT is meant to support humans, not replace them.

We all know that privacy is a big deal when it comes to AI, but it's not the only thing to be careful about. ChatGPT is powerful but it's not a replacement for human intelligence. It should be seen as a tool that helps us in our tasks and decision-making, not a substitute for our expertise.

In this chapter, we will look at the capabilities of ChatGPT while recognizing its limits. We will also see how important our human intelligence and critical thinking are in using AI effectively. Finding this balance will help us make the most of ChatGPT's power without worrying about losing our place in the world.

Limitations of ChatGPT

Before heading straight into the limitations of ChatGPT, let's quickly recap its advantages, which we covered earlier:

1. Simulates and Generates Human-Like Conversation

ChatGPT is a powerful tool that can engage in realistic interactions, making conversations feel like you're talking to a real human. Whether you're seeking assistance, brainstorming ideas, or simply engaging in friendly banter, ChatGPT can simulate a back-and-forth exchange that mirrors human conversation.

2. Built on the Advanced GPT Model and Language Fluency

ChatGPT is built upon the GPT (Generative Pre-trained Transformer) model, which helps it understand and use language well. It can come up with responses that make sense and sound natural, just like a language expert. It knows the right words to say and responds in a way that feels authentic and natural.

3. Scalable and Open to Fine-Tuning

ChatGPT is scalable and can get better over time. It can be fine-tuned to enhance performance and align better for specific uses or domains. It's like a smart robot that can keep learning and improving. It was designed to be adaptable to become more intelligent as technology advances.

4. Adaptability and Multiple Applications

ChatGPT is like a jack-of-all-trades! It can be used in many different ways for different things. ChatGPT's versatility allows it to be used in various sectors, from customer service chatbots and virtual assistants to creative writing prompts and educational tools. This makes it a valuable resource across different industries, offering tailored solutions.

5. Supports Integration with Plug-Ins for Extensions

ChatGPT supports integration with plug-ins for extensions to expand its functionality. These plug-ins are extra add-ons that make ChatGPT even more powerful and versatile. With them, ChatGPT can do all sorts of amazing stuff to meet your specific needs. For example, you can integrate external knowledge sources to make ChatGPT smart and well-informed. Or, you can add specialized functionalities to tailor the conversations just how you like them.

Understanding the Disadvantages of ChatGPT

One of the most concerning limitations to the use of ChatGPT is the issue of privacy and security. Imagine chatting with ChatGPT, sharing your innermost thoughts and secrets, and then suddenly, it hits you—Who's on the other side of this virtual conversation?

While OpenAI takes data privacy seriously, there's always a small chance that sensitive information could be exposed. ChatGPT needs data to learn from, including the text of the conversations it engages in. It's like walking a tightrope—balancing the advantages of personalized responses with safeguarding user privacy.

Another limitation is the potential for biased responses. Despite being a master of language, ChatGPT is still a product of its training data. And, let's face it, the internet is a wild jungle of biased information. There's a chance that ChatGPT's responses may carry some of that bias, too. It's not intentionally trying to be unfair, but rather, it's reflecting the imperfections of the data it was fed. This can generate responses that unintentionally favor one perspective over another.

Here's some more detail on those and other limitations:

1. Limited Knowledge

One of the most notable disadvantages of ChatGPT is limited knowledge. This is evident when using ChatGPT for researching a subject that needs up-to-date information.

Imagine you're a researcher trying to gather the most recent data on a cutting-edge field. You turn to ChatGPT with excitement, hoping to get the latest information and findings. However, you discover that ChatGPT's knowledge is only based on information before September 2021. It's like wanting to know who won the latest championship match but only being able to find out who won two years ago.

The limitation of knowledge in ChatGPT can be quite frustrating, especially in fast-paced fields. For instance, in AI, breakthroughs and advancements are happening all the time. If you rely solely on ChatGPT for your AI research, you might miss out on the latest models, algorithms, and innovations.

Let's consider an example outside the tech realm. Let's say you're interested in studying climate change and its impact on endangered species in 2023. You turn to ChatGPT to gather recent data and news articles, but unfortunately, the model can't provide you with information beyond its last update in September 2021. You could be missing out on crucial reports, research papers, and conservation efforts that occurred afterward.

This limitation can significantly affect researchers, journalists, and anyone seeking the most up-to-date information. The world constantly evolves, and discoveries can reshape our understanding of various topics. Not being able to access the latest data might hinder the progress of your research or lead to outdated conclusions.

2. Difficulty Handling Ambiguity

Handling ambiguity is no easy feat for anyone, even ChatGPT. It's a great tool for generating human-like responses, but it can sometimes struggle with vague queries.

When faced with ambiguous queries, ChatGPT relies on its training data to provide an appropriate response. However, this can lead to biased outputs because the data it's trained on might contain societal biases. For instance, if the model was trained on text that exhibited gender or racial bias, it might produce responses reflecting those biases.

Let's take an example to understand the challenge of ambiguity better. Consider the query: "Should I invest my money in stocks?" The response to this question can vary greatly depending on the user's financial situation, risk tolerance, and investment goals. ChatGPT might give a generic answer like, "Investing in stocks can offer good returns, but it also carries some risks," which isn't particularly helpful for a specific user.

Also, imagine asking ChatGPT, "What is the best diet?" This is quite an ambiguous question since the "best" diet might vary based on individual needs, health conditions, and personal preferences. ChatGPT might respond with a general diet plan, but it might not be your most suitable option.

Similarly, when discussing sensitive topics like politics or social issues, ChatGPT might provide responses that may lean toward certain biases in the data it was trained on. If the training data is biased toward a specific political ideology, the AI's responses might reflect that bias, even if unintentionally.

To address these challenges, you should ask specific and well-defined questions. Instead of asking, "What's the best career choice for me?" you can rephrase it as, "What are the advantages and disadvantages of pursuing a career in software engineering?" This way, the model will more likely provide a focused response.

It's important to remember that ChatGPT cannot replace human judgment. When making important decisions, you should approach its responses critically and cross-reference information from reliable sources.

3. Ambiguity and Inaccuracies

ChatGPT is not a magical oracle with all-encompassing knowledge. Instead, it relies solely on the data fed into its digital brain.

This means that ChatGPT can produce some pretty mind-blowing responses, but it's not flawless. Ambiguities and inaccuracies may sometimes creep into its answers. If you come across something that seems a bit off or unclear, don't fret! It's just a friendly reminder that our beloved AI is still a learning machine and might occasionally stumble.

Don't get me wrong, ChatGPT is pretty good at what it does. But to get the most out of ChatGPT's capabilities, you need to be open to its brilliance and occasional quirks.

ChatGPT can have biases in how it operates, which fall into five categories. The first two come from the input it receives. The third and fourth types are inherent in the AI software. The fifth bias appears in the users themselves. These are:

- **Sample Bias:** This bias comes from the limited data used to train the AI. Since only a specific group of people generates the content, the AI might not fully represent diverse perspectives.
- **Programmatic Morality Bias:** The software company introduces this bias to align ChatGPT with what is socially acceptable. It can influence the AI's responses to align with certain values. It aims to put in opinions seen as "socially correct," making ChatGPT fit in well with most users.
- **Ignorance Bias:** Users sometimes assume ChatGPT has deductive reasoning abilities due to its vast knowledge. However, it can only provide answers based on existing data and not reason through new questions.
- **Overton Window Bias:** ChatGPT has a bias called "Overton Window Bias," where it goes beyond what's considered appropriate in its knowledge base. It avoids

controversial topics and lacks the ability to know what is true. This can lead to problems when discussing controversial subjects, as its responses may not always be accurate. ChatGPT's output may repeat false information, and this makes it unreliable.

- **Deference Bias:** When people trust AI too much, we see three levels of "deference bias." The first is automation bias, where people rely too much on the technology's accuracy due to their heavy workloads. The second is authority bias: people granting AI political or intellectual authority influenced by recent challenges and our tendency to follow external authority. The third and most concerning is stress coercion, when people view AI as an authority and passionately defend it as a perfect entity. This might be influenced by the stressful Covid-19 pandemic and Big Tech's role in our lives during lockdowns. It's worrying that many people have become overly reliant on AI and surrendered their intellectual abilities to it.

The Effect and Impact When People Trust ChatGPT Too Much

ChatGPT's capabilities are undoubtedly amazing, but several consequences can arise when people place excessive trust in it. These may include:

- **Misinformation Spread:** ChatGPT relies on the data it has been exposed to, and it doesn't possess the ability to fact-check or verify information. If you accept everything ChatGPT says, misinformation and inaccuracies could spread.

- **Critical-Thinking Erosion:** Relying too heavily on ChatGPT for information may lead to a decline in critical-thinking skills. You may accept answers without questioning or exploring alternative information. Remember that ChatGPT is a tool and not an all-knowing oracle.
- **Lack of Human Connection:** Relying heavily on AI interactions may reduce human interactions, affecting social skills and emotional connections.
- **Privacy and Security Concerns:** Entrusting sensitive information to ChatGPT might raise privacy and security issues. It's important to take caution and be mindful of the information you share.
- **Dependency on AI for Decision-Making:** Over-reliance on ChatGPT for decision-making, especially in critical situations, can be risky. Human judgment and expertise remain irreplaceable in complex situations.

Bias in Natural Language Processing Model (NLP)

The natural language processing model allows ChatGPT to understand and process language like humans do. However, despite its capabilities, the natural language processing model is not immune to biases.

These biases stem from the data it learns from, sourced from human creators who may possess certain biases. Also, the system's design can introduce biases that can lead to incomplete or inaccurate information.

Now, let's get into some eye-opening examples of bias in ChatGPT. Imagine asking ChatGPT about a particular profession, and it responds with gender-specific language, assuming only one gender is associated with that job. For instance, when it was used to review job applicants' resumes, it favored female candidates because of the past underrepresentation of women in the data.

There have been accusations of political bias as well. When asked to write like different media outlets, ChatGPT refused to mimic the style of the *New York Post* but complied easily with CNN's style. There are claims that the model is more likely to flag negative comments about certain groups, like liberals, women, gays, and African Americans. However, these biases are not intentional on the part of the model developers but rather a result of the data used for training.

What Is the Root Cause of Bias in ChatGPT?

Our world is far from being bias-free, and those biases tend to sneak into the data used to train ChatGPT. To put it simply, the root cause of bias in ChatGPT lies in the data it was fed during its training. These data come from the internet, from articles, books, forums, and tweets to human-generated content. As diverse as it may seem, it still reflects the biases that exist in our society.

Now, let's talk about real-life examples. Take a look at a scenario where ChatGPT is asked to describe the ideal profession for a nurse. It might respond with a biased view, suggesting a female nurse without even considering male nurses. This doesn't mean ChatGPT is intentionally sexist—it just reflects the biases it has inadvertently learned from the data. Similarly, ChatGPT may unknowingly echo negative sentiments it has encountered in its training when discussing a certain culture or ethnicity.

Concerns and Issues of Ethical Importance

It's no secret that ChatGPT is a game-changer when it comes to brainstorming and finding solutions to problems. When used responsibly, it can improve productivity and creativity.

But here's where the ethical tightrope comes into play. The line between productivity boost and potential cheating lies in how we approach its usage. ChatGPT should never be a substitute for our original thoughts and efforts. Relying solely on AI to create academic papers, essays, or work projects can rob you of your learning process and personal growth.

Let's face it: the temptation to use this AI as a shortcut to academic or professional success can be all too real. Letting ChatGPT do the heavy lifting may be tempting, but you must remember that true growth and learning come from putting in the effort and engaging with your tasks wholeheartedly.

Using ChatGPT to support your journey is one thing, but relying on it to bypass hard work is another. Creativity, learning, and productivity thrive when you challenge yourself and tackle problems head-on. ChatGPT should never replace unique human touch and ingenuity.

How do we strike the perfect balance? Use ChatGPT as your trusty sidekick, but don't let it overshadow your abilities and potential. Use it to spark ideas, refine concepts, and complement your creative process. See it as a collaborator, not a replacement for your efforts.

ChatGPT as Therapist

Using ChatGPT for therapy has also become increasingly popular due to its accessibility and anonymity. People find solace in sharing their deepest thoughts and emotions with ChatGPT, believing it offers a safe and judgment-free space. However, there are potential pitfalls to it.

The risk here lies in the fact that you might divulge sensitive and personal information to ChatGPT without realizing that others could store and access your data. The last thing you would want is for your private therapy sessions to end up in the wrong hands.

Real therapists provide empathetic responses in their approach to each individual. Since ChatGPT's responses are based on the data it was trained on, their responses may include biased or inaccurate information. This could lead to harmful advice or promote harmful beliefs, particularly when dealing with sensitive mental health issues.

Potential Legal Implications

ChatGPT doesn't create original content out of thin air. It's not some magical wordsmith like Shakespeare; instead, it relies solely on the information that has been fed into its system.

And here's where things can get dicey from a legal perspective. Imagine using ChatGPT to make important decisions, like legal advice or medical diagnoses. If its responses are biased-based, it could lead to serious consequences. Legal matters are no joke; getting the wrong information could be seriously detrimental.

But wait, there's more. Since ChatGPT relies on historical data for its knowledge, it might not be up to date with the latest laws or regulations. To make matters worse, ChatGPT isn't just learning from textbooks or law journals. It gobbles up everything it finds online. You can imagine how this wide-ranging diet might result in some less-than-reliable responses. This is not exactly what you want when seeking precise legal or medical advice.

This isn't to say that ChatGPT is entirely useless in the legal realm. When used responsibly, with human oversight and awareness of its limitations, it can still provide useful insights. However, relying solely on its responses without careful consideration could land you a bit of a legal problem.

Treading Forward With Caution

Now that we have looked at the negative impact of ChatGPT, there is a need to tread with caution. ChatGPT is impressive but not perfect. Always cross-check the information with reliable sources before taking its responses as gospel truth. Here is how to make the most out of ChatGPT like a pro:

1. Be Clear and Specific

When interacting with ChatGPT, be clear and specific in your requests. The more precise you are, the better the model can understand your needs and respond accurately. Avoid long sentences and try to break down complex questions into simpler ones.

Example: Instead of asking, "Can you give me a detailed explanation of quantum physics?" try, "What are the fundamental principles of quantum physics?"

2. Experiment and Iterate

ChatGPT learns from its interactions, so feel free to experiment and iterate with your prompts. If the initial response isn't quite what you were looking for, don't worry. Adjust your question or provide more context to guide the model toward the desired outcome.

Example: If you ask, "Tell me a joke," and the response isn't hilarious, try something like, "Can you share a punny joke about cats?"

3. Give Context and Background

Provide some background information to get more personalized and relevant responses. This helps ChatGPT understand your specific situation and tailor its answers accordingly.

Example: Instead of asking, "How do I bake a cake?" provide context like, "I want to bake a chocolate cake for my friend's birthday, but I'm a beginner in baking."

4. Control the Tone

You have the power to set the tone of the conversation with ChatGPT. If you want a formal response, be polite and use appropriate language. For a more casual chat, you can be a bit more laid-back.

Example: To get a formal response about the weather, ask, "Could you please provide the weather forecast for tomorrow?" For a casual response, try, "What's the weather gonna be like tomorrow?"

5. Verify Information

ChatGPT doesn't have real-time access to information. Verifying critical information from reliable sources is always a good idea before making decisions based solely on ChatGPT's responses.

Example: If ChatGPT provides a recipe for an allergy-friendly dish, double-check with a trusted recipe website to ensure it's safe.

Measuring, Detecting, and Reducing Bias in ChatGPT

ChatGPT may require some time to address bias in its responses. However, you can take some measures to tackle this issue:

- Conduct thorough research and don't solely rely on ChatGPT when making significant decisions. Use examples that imagine different scenarios to understand things better.
- Many individuals are urging OpenAI to disclose the algorithm employed by ChatGPT to provide information. This transparency would aid users in understanding how the model operates and, more importantly, how it creates responses to queries.
- ChatGPT is currently being investigated for potentially using sensitive private data. This consideration should be kept in mind while using the program, as it may impact the answers received.
- Government officials in the United States and Europe are considering regulating ChatGPT. While these regulations could have both good and bad effects, you should keep up to date as the details unfold.

How Have Users Successfully Addressed Bias in ChatGPT?

Most users address bias in ChatGPT by maintaining clear boundaries and ensuring that bias doesn't creep into the conversations.

You can define specific guidelines and expectations that align with your values and principles. This way, ChatGPT helps you streamline tasks without compromising the quality of your interaction.

Users also take the approach of verifying each piece of information provided by ChatGPT. You should cross-reference the responses to ensure you have accurate and reliable information at hand.

When dealing with gender neutrality in job descriptions on ChatGPT, many users use gender-neutral language to ensure that job postings appeal to diverse applicants. This includes using gender-neutral job descriptions and stripping away words that lean toward a particular gender. This opens up opportunities for everyone and creates a welcoming environment where all candidates feel valued for their skills and qualifications.

By adopting these strategies, you can harness the potential of ChatGPT while minimizing bias and promoting fairness.

The Future of Bias in ChatGPT

ChatGPT comes with its limitations. One such limitation is that ChatGPT draws its information from human sources. And, as you may know, humans are not perfect; they carry with them biases.

Now, you might be wondering, "What does this mean for the future of ChatGPT?" Biases may persist, but they can be minimized and addressed over time. It's a collaborative effort between governments, activists, and developers that holds the key to refining ChatGPT.

Governments can play a crucial role by setting regulations and guidelines that ensure transparency and accountability in AI development. This would encourage responsible AI implementation and minimize any potential biases.

Developers are continuously fine-tuning and improving ChatGPT to reduce biases and make it more reliable and equitable. They can identify and address potential biases through careful analysis and data scrutiny.

The Implication of Its Use

Two significant areas where ChatGPT falls short are its limited creativity and lack of emotional understanding. ChatGPT lacks the innate creativity that only human minds can possess. Human creativity is driven by emotions, experiences, and the ability to think beyond patterns.

When it comes to emotional understanding, ChatGPT might not fully understand the depth of human emotions. Sure, it can analyze language patterns and produce responses, but it doesn't genuinely empathize or connect emotionally with you.

This shows that ChatGPT cannot take over jobs and businesses entirely, but it can help with productivity. You can delegate repetitive tasks such as drafting emails, creating content, or brainstorming ideas to ChatGPT. This frees up your time to focus on tasks that require human creativity and emotional understanding.

With ChatGPT, you have more mental space to spare so you can explore ideas, experiment with new concepts, and think outside the box. Also, ChatGPT can serve as a collaborative tool. You can use it to refine your ideas, expand your knowledge, and overcome creative blocks.

It is important to know that technology, no matter how advanced, is a complement to human abilities rather than a substitute. Knowing this can help you wield its power, using it as a springboard for efficiency.

Key Takeaway

- ChatGPT can be used to boost productivity and efficiency in mundane tasks, making time for more creative work.
- ChatGPT may not replace human creativity, but it can serve as a tool to collaborate with and complement

human minds, sparking fresh ideas and providing unique perspectives.

- Understanding the boundaries of ChatGPT allows you to use it more effectively, maximizing its potential as a support tool rather than a replacement for human skills.

What Next?

With an appreciation for the power and limitations of ChatGPT, we now shift our focus to its application in the workplace. In the next chapter, we will explore how ChatGPT is making its waves in various professional settings, changing how we work and interact with technology.

ChatGPT is set to redefine the workplace landscape, from streamlining tasks and improving productivity to enhancing communication and collaboration. Now, we will uncover real-world examples of how businesses and professionals are integrating ChatGPT into their daily operations to witness its impact on efficiency and innovation.

5. ChatGPT in the Workplace

L et's say you have a work partner by your side, one that
   never tires, never complains, and always has a wealth of
information at their fingertips. Well, that partner is ChatGPT.
According to a Korn Ferry recent survey of professionals across
industries, 46% of people already use ChatGPT to elevate their
work game. But what makes ChatGPT different?

From marketing wizards to data experts, people across all
industries use ChatGPT at their workplaces. It's not just a
luxury anymore; it's a necessity in this digital world. According
to Korn Ferry, over 80% of surveyed professionals agree that
ChatGPT is a legitimate and beneficial tool. It has taken over
the hearts and minds of many, proving its worth in the real
world.

As we saw in the previous chapter, ChatGPT has its limitations,
but it's hard to ignore the advantages it brings to the table. Sure,
many fear it will replace human jobs or lead to a less personal

touch in our work interactions, but the truth lies in its application.

When used wisely, ChatGPT becomes the perfect digital partner, working hand in hand with human creativity and intelligence. With ChatGPT by your side, you can tackle routine tasks, crunch data, and even generate content, allowing time for higher-level thinking. No more mind-numbing tasks; instead, you can welcome a fresh wave of creativity into your daily work life.

In this chapter, we'll talk about how you can use ChatGPT in the workplace and go into its ability to ignite creativity. As we continue, you will discover the advantages of using ChatGPT at work and learn how to integrate it effectively into your daily routines. At the end of this chapter, you'll be equipped to use ChatGPT to make strides in your professional career.

Effective Ways ChatGPT Can Boost Productivity and Creativity in the Workplace

ChatGPT can work wonders in helping you at work and spark creativity in your career. Here are some effective ways ChatGPT can make a real difference, whatever your field:

Marketing & Advertising

ChatGPT can be your guide in crafting compelling copy and ad content. You can use ChatGPT to brainstorm catchy slogans, refine social media posts, generate creative ideas on demand,

and save time and effort. Let's look at how ChatGPT can help you do this:

1. Refining Social Media Posts

Scenario: A social media manager needs to create engaging posts for an upcoming product promotion but is running short on time.

Sample Prompt: "Help me create an attention-grabbing social media post to promote our limited-time discount on fitness apparel."

2. Creating Engaging Email Subject Lines

Scenario: An email marketer wants to increase the open rates for their latest newsletter.

Sample Prompt: "Provide attention-grabbing subject lines for our monthly newsletter focused on health and wellness."

3. Crafting Engaging Video Scripts

Scenario: A video content producer wants to create compelling scripts for a series of brand videos.

Sample Prompt: "Help me draft a product demo video script highlighting versatility and ease of use."

Other Sample Prompts for Marketing & Advertising

- "Assist me in refining the ad copy for our travel agency's latest vacation package."
- "Suggest a compelling call-to-action for our email marketing campaign."

- "Generate creative ideas for a captivating billboard advertisement promoting our restaurant."
- "Come up with promotional ideas for our upcoming product launch event."

Content Creation and Writing

You can use ChatGPT to overcome writer's block and improve your creativity. You can create blog topics, outline articles, and explore new perspectives using ChatGPT as a co-writer or idea generator. Let's look at practical ways you can do this:

1. Blog Post Ideas

Scenario: Imagine you're a passionate travel blogger struggling to develop new post ideas. ChatGPT can help!

Sample Prompts: "Can you suggest topics for a travel blog focused on off-the-beaten-path destinations?"

2. Writing Engaging Introductions

Scenario: You're a food writer and are running out of ways to create interest in diet articles. You can use ChatGPT to get inspired.

Sample Prompts: "Can you help me create an attention-grabbing introduction for an article about healthy eating?"

3. Social Media Content

Scenario: You need words to go with your Instagram uploads from a recent trip, but you don't have time to think up any one-liners. Use ChatGPT for quick ideas.

Sample Prompts: "Can you suggest witty captions for my travel photos?"

Other Writing Sample Prompts

- "Assist me in writing an introduction for my photography portfolio."
- "Generate content ideas for my DIY home improvement blog."
- "Create an outline for a comprehensive guide on digital marketing."
- "Help me write product descriptions for our new fashion collection."

Software Development and Coding

When it comes to coding and development, you can use ChatGPT as a teammate. It can assist with debugging code, suggesting algorithms, and explaining complex programming concepts. As a developer, ChatGPT can help you solve problems efficiently. Let's look at how:

1. Code Refactoring

Scenario: A software developer is working on a complex codebase and wants to improve its readability and maintainability. They can use ChatGPT to get suggestions for code refactoring.

Sample Prompt: "Can you provide me with some ideas to refactor this code snippet to make it more efficient and easier to understand?"

2. Troubleshooting Bugs

Scenario: A software engineer encounters a persistent bug in their code and needs help debugging the issue. They can use ChatGPT to get insights into possible causes and solutions.

Sample Prompt: "I've been trying to find the bug in this section of my code for hours. Any suggestions on where I should look and how to fix it?"

3. Integration with External APIs

Scenario: A software developer is integrating their application with external APIs and facing challenges with data parsing. They can use ChatGPT to get suggestions on handling API responses.

Sample Prompt: "I'm working on integrating an API, but I'm stuck parsing the response data. Any tips on how to efficiently handle API responses in my code?"

Other Sample Prompts for Software Development

- "I'm learning Python. Can you provide me with beginner-friendly exercises to practice loops and conditionals?"
- "I want to build a chatbot for my website. What key steps and technologies should I consider for this project?"
- "I'm interested in learning about machine-learning algorithms. Can you give me a brief overview of decision trees and their applications?"

- "I'm struggling with database design. Can you provide some best practices and tips to design an efficient database schema?"

Design and UX/UI

As a designer and user experience expert, you can tap into ChatGPT's creativity to explore new design concepts and user interfaces. ChatGPT can generate design inspirations, propose color palettes, and even streamline the design process. Here's how:

1. Color Palette Suggestions

Scenario: As a graphic designer, you are working on a new branding project for a fashion company. You want a color palette that reflects their eco-friendly values.

Sample Prompt: "Suggest a color palette representing sustainability and nature for a fashion brand."

2. Drafting Wireframes

Scenario: You are a UX designer tasked with redesigning an e-commerce website to improve user experience. You want to create wireframes for the homepage.

Sample Prompt: "Help me draft wireframes for an e-commerce website homepage focusing on intuitive navigation and product discovery."

3. Design Trends in E-Commerce

Scenario: As a UX/UI designer for an online car brand, you want to stay updated on the latest design trends in e-commerce.

Sample Prompt: "What are the current design trends in e-commerce websites, especially for car brands?"

Other Sample Prompts for Design

- "Provide ideas for a user-friendly navigation menu for an e-commerce website selling home decor products."
- "Generate a layout for a mobile app that promotes eco-friendly practices and sustainability."
- "Suggest an animation concept for an e-learning platform that enhances user engagement during courses."
- "Help me create a user-friendly checkout process for an online bookstore, emphasizing ease of payment and quick order confirmation."

Project Management

Managing projects can be overwhelming, but ChatGPT can lighten the load. It can help you generate meeting agendas, draft progress reports, and even offer suggestions for task allocation in efficient project workflows. Here are some suggestions:

1. Generating Meeting Agendas

Scenario: As a project manager, you have a team meeting coming up, and you want to create a well-structured agenda to ensure a productive discussion.

Sample Prompt: "I need help creating an agenda for our upcoming project review meeting. Can you suggest the main topics we should cover and any key discussion points?"

2. Resource Allocation and Task Assignment

Scenario: You have a new project with a limited budget and must allocate resources effectively while ensuring each team member has a clear task assignment.

Sample Prompt: "I have a new project, but resources are limited. Can you provide recommendations on allocating resources and assigning tasks based on team members' skills?"

3. Project Budgeting and Cost Control

Scenario: You are working on a project with a fixed budget and need assistance developing a cost-control plan to avoid over-spending.

Sample Prompt: "I'm managing a project with a tight budget. Can you provide tips on effective cost-control measures to ensure we stay within budget without compromising quality?"

Other Sample Prompts for Project Management

- "Please create a project timeline for an upcoming product launch."
- "Assist me in identifying potential risks in our software development project."
- "Can you help me draft a project proposal for a new client pitch?"
- "Provide suggestions on how to improve team collaboration and communication."

Education and Training

In the education sector, ChatGPT can serve as an interactive learning companion. It can generate quiz questions, explain complex topics, and create interactive study materials for students and teachers. Here's how:

1. Quiz Question Generator

Scenario: A teacher wants to create engaging quizzes for their students.

Sample Prompt: "Generate five multiple-choice questions on photosynthesis for my biology class."

2. Vocabulary Building

Scenario: An ESL (English as a Second Language) learner wants to practice and expand their vocabulary.

Sample Prompt: "Provide me with ten advanced English words, their meanings, and usage in sentences."

3. Practice Math Problems

Scenario: A high school student wants to practice solving algebraic equations.

Sample Prompt: "Generate three algebraic equations with variables on both sides for me to solve."

Customer Support

ChatGPT can help provide responses to common customer queries, providing instant support and freeing up space to focus on more brain-demanding issues. Here's how:

1. Personalized Customer Interactions

Scenario: You have just read an article saying that customers appreciate a personalized touch in their interactions with customer support. ChatGPT can help you craft personalized responses by analyzing customer data and understanding their needs.

Sample Prompt: "How can I address a customer who has just purchased our premium subscription?"

2. Handling Escalated Complaints

Scenario: A customer has escalated their complaint as they are dissatisfied with the customer support they have received so far. ChatGPT can help you draft empathetic and reassuring responses to ensure you address the customer's concerns.

Sample Prompt: "How should I respond to a customer who is unhappy with our service and demanding a refund?"

3. Multilingual Support

Scenario: You are in an international marketplace now. A Spanish customer has contacted you, and you are unfamiliar with the language. ChatGPT can act as a translator to communicate with customers in various languages.

Sample Prompt: "How do I greet a customer in Spanish who has reached out for support?"

Sample Prompts for you to Try Out

- "What are the key features of our latest product?"
- "Can you help me troubleshoot a connectivity issue with our device?"
- "How can I handle a customer who is having difficulty accessing their account?"
- "Can you provide me with a sample script to handle a customer complaint about a delayed shipment?"

Human Resources and Recruitment

Recruitment and HR professionals can rely on ChatGPT to assist with writing compelling job descriptions, screening candidates with predefined questions, and providing onboarding information for new hires. Here's how ChatGPT can help:

1. Writing Job Descriptions

Scenario: A human resources manager is tasked with creating a compelling job description for a new marketing manager position.

Sample Prompt: "I need help crafting a job description for a marketing manager role. The ideal candidate should have experience in digital marketing and a proven track record of successful campaign management. Can you help me develop a captivating and informative job description?"

2. Candidate Screening

Scenario: A recruitment specialist is going through a large pool of applicants for an entry-level customer support position and needs assistance screening potential candidates.

Sample Prompt: "I have hundreds of resumes for the customer support role, and I need to identify the most qualified candidates. Can you help me create a set of screening questions to assess their communication skills, problem-solving abilities, and customer-centric approach?"

3. Interview Questions

Scenario: An HR professional is preparing for an interview with a potential candidate for a sales position and needs help formulating relevant questions.

Sample Prompt: "I have an interview scheduled with a sales representative candidate. Can you assist me in crafting a list of behavioral and situational questions to assess their sales experience, negotiation skills, and ability to handle challenging situations?"

Other Sample Prompts for Human Resources

- "Generate a job description for a software engineer role focusing on front-end development skills."
- "Help me develop a set of interview questions to evaluate candidates for a project manager position."
- "Outline an onboarding checklist for new hires in our marketing department."
- "Create a performance evaluation template highlighting key performance indicators for sales representatives."

Financial Analysis and Reporting

ChatGPT can be very useful for financial analysts and accountants. It can help in data analysis, develop financial reports, and provide insights into market trends to make better financial decisions. Here's how:

1. Data Analysis Assistance

Scenario: A financial analyst wants to analyze a company's financial data to identify trends and key performance indicators (KPIs).

Sample Prompt: "I need help analyzing XYZ Company's financial data. Can you assist me in identifying the revenue growth and profit margin trends over the past three years?"

2. Generating Financial Reports

Scenario: An accountant must prepare a monthly financial report for the company's stakeholders.

Sample Prompt: "I have to create a comprehensive financial report summarizing our company's income statement, balance sheet, and cash flow statement for the past quarter. Can you help me draft the report?"

3. Market Analysis Insights

Scenario: A financial researcher wants to gain insights into market trends and competitor analysis.

Sample Prompt: "I'm researching the current market trends in the technology sector and need information on the top-performing tech companies and their market share. Can you provide me with some data and analysis?"

Other Sample Prompts for Financial Analysis

- "Please analyze the revenue and cost trends of ABC Corporation for the last five years and identify any patterns or fluctuations."
- "I'm researching the consumer goods industry. Can you generate a comparative analysis of the financial performance of three major companies in this sector?"
- "I'm considering investing in tech start-ups, but I need insights into their financial stability and growth prospects. Can you help me assess the financial health of three potential startup investments?"

- "I need to create a financial report for my department's budget presentation. Can you assist me in summarizing our expenses and revenue data for the past quarter?"

Healthcare and Research

Even in the medical field, ChatGPT has a role to play. It can aid healthcare professionals in diagnosing symptoms, researching medical literature, and suggesting treatment options based on scientific findings.

1. Diagnosis Assistance

Sample Prompt: "I'm a medical professional evaluating a patient with fever, cough, and fatigue symptoms. Can you help me narrow down possible diagnoses and suggest appropriate tests?"

2. Medical Literature Research

Sample Prompt: "I'm researching the effectiveness of a new drug for diabetes treatment. Can you provide me with recent studies and clinical trial results published in medical journals?"

3. Treatment Options for a Specific Condition

Sample Prompt: "I'm a physician seeking alternative treatment options for a patient with severe migraines who has not responded well to standard medications. Can you suggest some innovative therapies or approaches?"

4. Public Health Strategies

Sample Prompt: "I'm a public health officer tasked with designing an intervention to reduce obesity rates in our community. Can you provide evidence-based strategies and best practices used in similar successful programs?"

Other Sample Prompts for Healthcare & Research

- "I'm interested in learning about the current research on Alzheimer's disease. Can you suggest some reputable sources?"
- "I'm conducting research on genetic disorders. Can you help me find relevant case studies and genetic testing methods?"
- "Can you explain the mechanism of action for a specific medication used to treat depression?"
- "I need information on the long-term effects of concussions on athletes. Can you provide some insights?"

With ChatGPT as a versatile tool, professionals from all walks of life can use it to increase productivity at work. ChatGPT can help teams and individuals to reach new heights of success by streamlining tasks, suggesting new ideas, and providing useful information.

Microsoft and ChatGPT

Microsoft is taking big steps in adding artificial intelligence to its popular tools like Outlook, PowerPoint, Excel, and Word. Their goal is to simplify the way millions of users work every day.

Microsoft plans to introduce an AI "Co-pilot" to Microsoft 365 users. This is capable of editing, summarizing, creating, and comparing documents. With this feature, you can transcribe meeting notes while chatting on Skype, quickly get summarized email replies, request custom charts in Excel, and convert Word docs into PowerPoint presentations in a blink. These advancements promise to make workflows easier for Microsoft 365 users.

There is more! Microsoft is also introducing Business Chat to the digital world. It's like a super-smart assistant that understands and organizes all your data—emails, calendar events, documents, presentations, chats, and meetings—within Microsoft 365.

However, it's not just Microsoft in the AI race. Google, their rival, is also gearing up to integrate AI into their tools like Gmail, Sheets, and Docs.

The tech industry is buzzing with excitement as AI tools are changing how we work, shop, and live. And you know what? These developments will open doors of opportunities to those who can harness these tools.

Key Takeaway

In this chapter, we explored the practical and effective ways ChatGPT can boost productivity in the workplace across various professions and industries. We delved into how marketing, content creation, software development, design, project management, education, customer support, human resources, finance, and healthcare professionals can leverage ChatGPT to enhance their work processes and outcomes. Also, Microsoft's integration of ChatGPT into Word and Excel will bring AI-powered assistance directly to users' fingertips, simplifying tasks in all fields.

What Next?

Now that we have explored the impact of ChatGPT on individual productivity and creativity in various workplace scenarios, it's time to look further into its role in the business world. In the next chapter, we will explore how enterprises and professionals across various industries use ChatGPT to improve efficiency, decision-making, and customer engagement. From customer support to market research, ChatGPT can redefine how businesses operate, ensuring they stay ahead in the ever-evolving business world.

6. ChatGPT in Business

As a solopreneur, my days were always filled to the brim with endless tasks, deadlines, and a never-ending list of ideas to explore. It was tiring going through the same routine over and over again; I needed something that could make my work easier and boost my income. That's when I started using ChatGPT.

From the moment I integrated ChatGPT into my business, I felt an immediate shift in my workflow. The time-consuming process of writing compelling marketing copy became a breeze. With ChatGPT, I could create engaging content ideas and craft captivating email campaigns in less time. This allowed me to focus on other aspects of my business, like building client relationships and strategizing for growth.

But perhaps the most significant impact of ChatGPT was on my creativity. I was free from routine tasks; I had more mental space to think strategically about my business. ChatGPT also sparked innovative ideas that breathed new life into my products and services to capture my audience's attention and drive sales like never before.

As my business boomed, so did my income. My productivity led directly to increased revenue and a growing customer base. With ChatGPT by my side, I was able to achieve more in less time and chart a course to new heights. In this chapter, we will discuss the practical applications of ChatGPT in businesses, showing how it can significantly help you increase productivity and income.

Practical Ways to Use ChatGPT to Boost Productivity and Income in Your Business

Use ChatGPT as your Marketing Wizard

Gone are the days of endless buzz sessions and hours spent fine-tuning marketing materials. With ChatGPT, you can develop ideas, creative concepts, and persuasive messaging with just a few keystrokes. This tool can guide you through the marketing maze with unique strategies. Let's see how:

1. Market Trends and Insights

ChatGPT can scour the web for market trends and consumer insights. You can provide specific prompts like, "What are the emerging trends in the tech industry?" or, "What are the preferences of Gen Z consumers?" to get information that can help you develop sound marketing strategies and campaigns.

2. Competitor Analysis

Gaining a competitive edge is important for any business. With ChatGPT, you can ask for a thorough analysis of your competitors, like, "Compare our product features against Company X" or, "What marketing strategies does Company Y employ?" With ChatGPT's responses, you can tweak your marketing approach and stand out.

3. Customer Personal Development

Understanding your target audience is crucial in marketing. ChatGPT can assist in developing detailed customer personas. Simply ask for prompts like, "Create a customer persona for a fintech company target audience." ChatGPT will provide information to tailor your marketing messages accordingly.

4. Keyword Research

ChatGPT can perform keyword research for an effective SEO strategy. Use prompts such as: "Identify relevant keywords for luxury clothing category" or "What are the top search terms in the fashion industry?" ChatGPT's responses will help optimize your content and improve search engine rankings.

Other Sample Prompts for Marketing

- "Analyze consumer sentiment toward our brand on social media."
- "Create a customer persona for our luxury product line."
- "Provide insights on market trends for health and wellness products."

- "We are launching a new fitness product aimed at young professionals. Can you provide insights on potential customer segments and content ideas to target them effectively?"

ChatGPT as Your Finance Maestro

Finance teams deal with mountains of data daily. With ChatGPT, you can simplify financial analysis and reporting. From preparing financial statements to crunching complex numbers, ChatGPT can assist in crafting detailed reports and interpreting financial data with ease. This saves time and reduces the chance of errors.

1. Financial Reporting Made Easy

Imagine you have to create detailed financial reports regularly; that's stressful and tiring. With ChatGPT, you can simply provide the necessary data and ask it to create the report. Whether it's balance sheets, income statements, or cash flow analysis, ChatGPT can analyze the numbers and deliver the report in no time.

Sample Prompt: "Create a monthly balance sheet report for Q3 2023 based on the provided financial data."

2. Investment Research and Analysis

When researching potential investment opportunities, ChatGPT can be your research assistant. It can analyze market trends, study historical data, and provide information on specific companies or industries.

Sample Prompt: "Analyze the performance of XYZ Company's stock over the last five years and provide an overview of potential investment risks."

3. Financial Forecasting and Budgeting

ChatGPT can assist in financial forecasting and budgeting to boost your business's future financial performance. ChatGPT can analyze historical data and market trends to aid decision-making, whether sales projections or expense forecasts.

Sample Prompt: "Create a budget forecast for the next fiscal year, taking into account historical revenue and expense data."

4. Financial Presentations and Reports

Creating engaging financial presentations can be time-consuming. ChatGPT can help draft slides, summaries, and visuals to support your financial presentations.

Sample Prompt: "Create a PowerPoint presentation summarizing our financial performance for the board meeting."

Other Sample Prompts for Finance

- "Forecast our cash flow for the next quarter based on our historical data."
- "Analyze the financial performance of our top three competitors over the past year."
- "Recommend investment options for diversifying our portfolio."
- "Explain the impact of inflation on our purchasing power."

- "Assess the financial risks associated with launching a new product."

Innovative Product Development

ChatGPT can be your guide when it comes to innovation. It can ideate on new product features, explore customer needs and preferences, and predict market trends to manage product development efforts. You can use ChatGPT to stay ahead of the innovation curve and create groundbreaking solutions that resonate with your customers. Here is how:

1. Prototyping and Design

ChatGPT can help in the initial stages of design and prototyping. Prompt it with questions like, "What should our product's user interface look like?" or, "Suggest design elements for our prototype."

2. Ideation and Brainstorming

Use prompts like, "Generate new product ideas for our target market," and watch as ChatGPT generates different concepts you can try. Your team can work on these unique ideas and refine them into actionable plans.

3. User Feedback Analysis

Feedback from users is a goldmine of information for product development. With prompts like, "Analyze customer feedback on our latest product release," ChatGPT can summarize and categorize user responses, allowing you to address your customer's concerns and improve their product experience.

4. Content Creation

ChatGPT can help create engaging content for product descriptions, marketing materials, and user guides. Use prompts like, "Write a compelling product description for our cosmetic product," ChatGPT will craft convincing narratives that captivate potential customers.

Other Sample Prompts for Product Development

- "What are the latest trends in wearable technology?"
- "Suggest innovative features for a smart home device."
- "Describe a user-friendly interface for a productivity app."
- "Describe an eco-friendly packaging solution for our new product line."
- "Compare our product's pricing strategy with our main competitor and identify potential adjustments."

Use ChatGPT as your Customer Support Champion

ChatGPT can be your aid in providing exceptional customer support. It can understand customer queries, respond accurately, handle routine inquiries, and free up your support team to focus on more important tasks. This means happier customers and a more efficient support team.

1. Personalized Responses

ChatGPT can help you build strong customer relationships by crafting personalized and heartfelt responses. This leads to higher customer retention rates.

Sample Prompt: "Draft a personalized response to a customer who had a positive experience with our product."

2. Automated FAQs

ChatGPT can generate FAQs about your product. This reduces the burden on the support team and allows your customers to find quick answers to common queries on their own.

Sample Prompt: "Create a list of FAQs and their answers for our website's support page."

3. Language Translation

ChatGPT helps you overcome language barriers with its multi-lingual support system. This allows you to communicate with customers from diverse backgrounds efficiently.

Sample Prompt: "Translate the customer's query from Italian to English."

4. Crisis Management Responses

In times of crisis, ChatGPT can quickly develop empathetic responses, assuring customers that their concerns are acknowledged.

Sample Prompt: "Provide a response template for customers affected by the recent service disruption."

Other Sample Prompts for Customer Support

- "Generate an apology email for a delayed order delivery."
- "Draft a response for a customer asking about our refund policy."
- "Provide a step-by-step guide for setting up our software on a new device."
- "Create a response template for handling customer complaints about damaged products."

HR and Recruitment

ChatGPT eases the burden on HR by automating the screening process for job applicants. It can review resumes, identify qualified candidates, and conduct preliminary interviews. This ensures a fair and unbiased selection process in your organization. ChatGPT can help streamline the process by crafting documents like employee handbooks or answering frequently asked questions for new hires.

1. Crafting Engaging Job Descriptions

ChatGPT can develop a well-written and compelling job description that attracts top talent by feeding it details about the role, required skills, and company culture.

Sample Prompt: "Help us create a captivating job description for a Senior Software Engineer position."

2. Screening and Shortlisting Candidates

ChatGPT can analyze resumes and match candidates based on specified criteria. This saves time in the initial screening process and ensures that only the most suitable candidates move forward.

Sample Prompt: "Review these resumes and shortlist candidates for the Sales Representative role."

3. Interview Question Preparation

HR teams can use ChatGPT to create a list of interview questions for specific job roles.

Sample Prompt: "Provide a set of behavioral interview questions to assess a candidate's problem-solving skills."

4. Employee Onboarding

ChatGPT can assist in creating onboarding materials for new hires, including welcome emails and orientation documents.

Sample Prompt: "Draft a comprehensive onboarding package for our new software engineer, covering key company policies and department overviews."

Other Sample Prompts for HR and Recruitment

- "Develop a set of questions to assess a candidate's adaptability and teamwork skill."
- "Help me create a job posting for a Customer Support Specialist focusing on empathetic communication and problem-solving skills."

- "Assist us in pre-screening applicants for a Graphic Designer role by asking about their design experience and preferred tools."
- "I need to conduct a second-round interview for a Marketing Manager. Generate a list of strategic marketing questions to evaluate their leadership skills."
- "Help us craft a rejection email that provides constructive feedback to candidates who did well."

Legal Insights

Legal teams can benefit from using ChatGPT to analyze and summarize legal documents. It can provide information, from contract reviews to researching case laws. As a lawyer or paralegal, here is how to use ChatGPT to your advantage:

Contract Review and Summarization

ChatGPT can help in analyzing lengthy contracts and legal documents. By providing a prompt like, "Please analyze and summarize the key terms of the contract between Company X and Company Y," ChatGPT can develop a summary highlighting important clauses and potential areas of concern.

Sample Prompt: "Please review this contract and concisely summarize the key terms and conditions."

Legal Research and Case Analysis

With ChatGPT's vast knowledge base, you can use it for your legal research. Prompting it with questions like, "Find recent case laws related to intellectual property disputes," can yield relevant results.

Sample Prompt: "Can you research recent case laws related to product liability in the healthcare industry?"

Regulatory Compliance Assistance

ChatGPT can keep the legal team updated on changing regulations and compliance requirements. A prompt such as: "Provide a summary of the recent changes in data protection laws," enables the team to address compliance issues.

Analyzing Legal Arguments

With ChatGPT, your team can gain a deeper understanding of legal arguments. It can help identify potential weaknesses, evaluate counterarguments, and support your team in building persuasive cases.

Sample Prompt: "Analyze the strengths and weaknesses of this legal argument in the pending litigation."

Other Sample Prompts for Legal Insights

- "Analyze and summarize the key provisions of the employment contract for John Doe, including termination clauses."
- "Research recent case laws related to copyright infringement in the digital content industry."
- "Provide a legal opinion on the potential liability of Company ABC in the recent product liability case."

- "Review the lease agreement for potential issues related to property maintenance responsibilities."
- "Identify any compliance requirements for conducting business operations in Country X."

Business Strategy

ChatGPT can be very useful when it comes to strategic planning. It can help you explore different scenarios, conduct SWOT analyses, and help in developing business plans. ChatGPT's knowledge base makes it an excellent resource for data-driven decision-making. Let's see how you can use this tool:

1. Ideation and Brainstorming

ChatGPT can serve as your collaborator in developing ideas to fuel your business strategy. It can provide new perspectives, explore different market opportunities, and suggest potential features or improvements for existing products.

Sample Prompt: "Come up with ideas for a new product or service that aligns with our company's vision and market trends."

2. SWOT Analysis

ChatGPT can identify your business's strengths, weaknesses, opportunities, and threats. It can provide information on market trends, customer preferences, and potential risks. This can help you develop an all-inclusive business strategy to increase your revenue.

Sample Prompt: "Conduct a SWOT analysis for an online fashion retail business."

3. Scenario Planning

ChatGPT can simulate different scenarios, considering factors like market dynamics, consumer behavior, and economic trends. You can make data-driven decisions with confidence by exploring potential outcomes.

Sample Prompt: "Explore various scenarios for entering a new market or launching a product."

4. Competitive Positioning

ChatGPT can help express your brand's unique selling points, stating key determiners that resonate with your target audience. It can craft compelling messaging that sets your business apart to ensure a strong position in the market.

Sample Prompt: "Develop a unique value proposition that differentiates our brand from competitors."

5. Crafting Business Proposals

ChatGPT can be your co-pilot when drafting business proposals.

Sample Prompt: "Generate a compelling business proposal for our new product launch, highlighting its unique selling points and potential market impact."

Other Sample Prompts for Business Strategy

- "Perform a detailed analysis of our target audience's preferences and buying behaviors."
- "Create a plan for entering the Asian market, considering cultural differences and local competition."
- "Provide information on potential partnerships or acquisitions to expand our market reach and competitive advantage."
- "Devise a contingency plan to navigate potential supply chain disruptions in times of crisis."
- "Evaluate the potential impact of emerging technologies on our business model and suggest adaptation strategies."

How Businesses are Incorporating ChatGPT to Improve Business Operations

In recent years, businesses have seen the potential of ChatGPT in improving and streamlining various systems to increase productivity and income. It is becoming a must-have tool—for everything from customer service to data analysis. Let's explore how businesses are incorporating ChatGPT to achieve their goals:

1. Customer Support and Engagement

ChatGPT helps in handling routine queries, providing person-alized recommendations, and troubleshooting common prob-lems while maintaining a human-like conversational experience. Businesses can build stronger customer loyalty and enhance customer satisfaction with ChatGPT on their side.

2. Data Analysis and Decision-Making

Businesses use ChatGPT to analyze customer sentiment, extract information from customer feedback, and analyze market trends. With ChatGPT's assistance, your business can increase operational efficiency and identify new opportunities by making data-driven decisions.

3. Content Generation and Marketing

ChatGPT is making big waves in content creation and marketing efforts. It can craft engaging blog posts, social media content, email newsletters, and ad copy. ChatGPT is helping businesses maintain a consistent online presence, attract more leads, and drive higher conversions.

4. Process Automation and Efficiency

Integrating ChatGPT with existing systems can help your business automate repetitive tasks and simplify internal processes. From scheduling meetings and managing appointments to handling administrative tasks, ChatGPT can reduce manual workload and allow employees to concentrate on other things.

5. Training and Onboarding

ChatGPT can also be used in employee training and onboarding processes. It can mimic real-world scenarios and interactive learning experiences. This helps your recruit get used to their roles faster.

6. Innovation and Ideation

Businesses are tapping into ChatGPT's creative potential to drive innovation and creativity. With ChatGPT as a brainstorming partner, you can come up with new product concepts and solve complex problems while stimulating creativity and collaboration.

Callback to the Importance of Fact-Checking and Revising

As we wrap up this chapter, we must address an aspect: the importance of fact-checking and revising ChatGPT's responses. ChatGPT is undoubtedly mind-blowing; you may have tried the above prompts and are surprised at its great responses. But here is a little reminder: ChatGPT is not an all-knowing oracle.

As we discussed earlier, exercising caution and human judgment in interpreting its output is important. ChatGPT is trained on large amounts of data; hence, it can produce errors or provide inaccurate information. Therefore, fact-checking and verifying its responses is very important, especially when dealing with legal matters where precision and accuracy are undebatable.

When drafting legal documents or making important business decisions, you should never solely rely on ChatGPT's output. It's always wise to consult legal experts and subject matter specialists to validate the information generated by ChatGPT.

Similarly, in any context, fact-checking ChatGPT's responses enhances the quality of the content and ensures it aligns with your company's values and objectives. Human input and creativity play a key role in refining ChatGPT's suggestions and tailoring them to the unique needs of your business.

You need to always remember that ChatGPT, regardless of how amazing it is, is a tool meant to complement human abilities and not to replace them. It can boost your productivity and inspire creativity, but your expertise is key in evaluating, refining, and applying ChatGPT's ideas. Use ChatGPT as a collaborative partner, working hand in hand with your team to achieve the best possible outcomes.

Key Takeaway

In this chapter, we explored the practical and effective ways ChatGPT can increase productivity and income in your business. We delved into real-life examples and scenarios where you can use ChatGPT as an asset, assisting in market research, strategic planning, competitive intelligence, and more. Integrating ChatGPT into business workflows can ease processes, improve efficiency, and ultimately lead to better business performance.

What Next?

As we continue our journey exploring the power of ChatGPT, our next chapter takes us into personal development. Beyond its business and workplace applications, ChatGPT can play a life-changing role in your growth and self-improvement. In this upcoming chapter, we will look at how ChatGPT can support personal development goals, whether improving communication skills, setting and achieving personal milestones, managing stress, or simply finding inspiration and motivation.

7. ChatGPT in Personal Development

I was speaking to my very close friend about ChatGPT. My initial thought was to spread the good news of how it has been helping me in my career; I didn't know he had also started using the tool. I will share his experience to show you that ChatGPT is beyond the four walls of your office. Its benefits can extend to your personal life.

Isaac is a very curious person. He is always looking for ways to level up his life. But he faced the usual challenges of juggling work, personal goals, and a never-ending to-do list. Little did he know that a change was about to enter his life—ChatGPT!

He was skeptical at first but decided to give it a try. As a digital marketer at heart, he often faces writer's block. But with ChatGPT by his side, he found a wellspring of inspiration. It never failed to impress and became his companion, always ready to work with him.

ChatGPT made interactions look like a conversation with a supportive friend. He would use this tool during late-night study sessions, buzz sessions for work projects, and moments of creative thinking.

But that's not all! ChatGPT has been an excellent life coach to him. He has used it in learning new habits and routines. With its motivational pep talks, he was able to form healthier habits.

From his life, I could say that ChatGPT has gone beyond just a tool; it's a companion, mentor, and confidant. The best part? ChatGPT has helped him develop lifelong learning for him to evolve and grow continually.

In this chapter, we will look into the possibilities of self-development with ChatGPT. You will learn about the advantages of using this tool in your life for personal and professional growth.

Practical Ways ChatGPT Can Improve Your Personal and Professional Life

Let's look at the ways ChatGPT can supercharge your daily routines and maximize your potential:

Personal Productivity Partner

ChatGPT is like having a digital assistant at your fingertips. It can help you stay organized by creating to-do lists and managing your schedule. It can also help in goal setting and tracking your progress, keeping you motivated and on top of your game. ChatGPT can provide suggestions, helping you make better decisions on your project, schedule, and others. Here's how it works:

1. Overcoming Procrastination

Scenario: Procrastination is a constant roadblock in your pursuits, and you need strategies to overcome this productivity killer.

Sample Prompt: "How can I beat procrastination and stay motivated to work on my hobby regularly? I need effective techniques to stay on track."

2. Balancing Screen Time

Scenario: You find yourself spending excessive time on social media and digital distractions. This can hinder your growth and prevent you from exploring new ideas.

Sample Prompt: "Help me reduce my screen time and create a healthier balance between online activities and pursuing my new hobby."

3. Time Management

Scenario: You need personalized time management tips and strategies to stay on track throughout the day.

Sample Prompt: "ChatGPT, how can I better manage my time to be more productive at work?"

Skill Development Support

Looking to learn a new skill or study a topic of interest? ChatGPT is your go-to knowledge companion. It can curate personalized learning resources, recommend online courses, and explain complex concepts. Just fire away with your questions; it will serve relevant information and resources like a seasoned expert.

1. Advancing Professional Skills

Scenario: Like my friend Isaac, you are career-driven, aiming to improve your professional skills. You want to take online courses, but with so many options, you are confused about which ones will benefit your career most.

Sample Prompt: "I'm looking to boost my professional skills through online courses. Can you suggest some courses that align with a marketing and project management career?"

2. Mastering a Specific Skill

Scenario: You've been eyeing that interesting skill, be it playing the guitar, learning to code, or cooking like a chef. It's time to unlock it with ChatGPT by your side.

Sample Prompt: "I've always wanted to learn how to play the guitar. Can you suggest a step-by-step learning plan and some helpful online tutorials?"

3. Personalized Learning Path

Scenario: You want to go into a particular field, but you're looking for a customized learning path. ChatGPT's got your back.

Sample Prompt: "I'm interested In psychology. Can you help with a list of books, podcasts, and courses to help me explore this field?"

Creative Muse

Have a creative block? ChatGPT can help you with imaginative ideas and writing prompts. ChatGPT can be your creative muse, whether you're an artist, writer, or someone who just loves exploring their creative side. It can provide you with ideas and help you overcome creative blocks.

1. The Writer's Block Dilemma

Scenario: You're a passionate writer, but lately, the writer's block has left you feeling uninspired. Your mind draws blanks, and you struggle to start that next chapter or write a captivating story.

Sample Prompt: "Help me brainstorm an interesting plot twist for my historical romance novel."

2. The Artist's Creative Stagnation

Scenario: You long to create captivating art pieces as an artist, but lately, you've hit a wall of stagnation. Your inspiration seems blank, and you're yearning to explore new artistic techniques.

Sample Prompt: "I'm looking to experiment with new art styles. Can you guide me through some contemporary art movements for inspiration?"

3. Exploring Creative Hobbies

Scenario: You want to explore new creative hobbies but don't know where to start.

Sample Prompt: "Recommend a beginner-friendly craft or DIY project to enhance my home decor."

Mental Health Buddy

Taking care of your mental well-being is important, and ChatGPT can lend a helping hand. With ChatGPT, you can engage in reflective conversations, practice mindfulness exercises, or receive supportive messages to maintain a positive outlook on life.

1. Managing Stress and Improving Sleep

Scenario: Stress and lack of sleep affect your overall well-being. You need strategies to manage stress and improve your sleep quality for a healthier lifestyle.

Sample Prompt: "I've been feeling stressed lately, and it's affecting my sleep. Can you recommend some relaxation techniques and bedtime routines to help me manage stress and sleep better?"

2. Boosting Self-Esteem

Scenario: You're struggling with low self-esteem and self-doubt, impacting your confidence and self-worth.

Sample Prompt: "I could use a confidence boost. Can you provide positive affirmations or self-love exercises to help me improve my self-esteem?"

3. Managing Emotions

Scenario: You find it challenging to handle intense emotions like anger, sadness, or frustration in a healthy way.

Sample Prompt: "I need some advice on managing my emotions better. How can I practice emotional regulation techniques to respond more calmly to situations?"

Language and Communication Improvement

Want to level up your communication game? ChatGPT can be your language tutor. It can help in improving your writing skills, grammar, and vocabulary. Practice conversing in different languages or fine-tune your public speaking abilities with ChatGPT.

1. Public Speaking Nerves

Scenario: Public speaking fills you with anxiety, and you want to feel more confident during presentations.

Sample Prompt: "I have a big presentation coming up, and I'm nervous about speaking in front of a crowd. Can you advise me on overcoming nervousness and delivering a compelling speech?"

2. Learning a New Language

Scenario: You've always wanted to learn a new language but don't know where to start or how to practice conversational skills.

Sample Prompt: "I want to learn Spanish, but I don't have anyone to practice with. Can you help me with my pronunciation and some basic conversational phrases?"

3. Improving Grammar and Vocabulary

Scenario: Your grammar and vocabulary could sound more polished and professional.

Sample Prompt: "I want to enhance my writing style by improving my grammar and vocabulary. Can you give me tips on how to expand my word choices and avoid common grammatical errors?"

4. Effective Communication in Conflict Resolution

Scenario: Communicating during conflicts can be challenging. ChatGPT can guide you on active listening and how to develop effective communication skills to resolve conflicts amicably.

Sample Prompt: "I had an argument with a friend. How can I approach them to discuss the issue and mend our relationship?"

Job Search and Career Advancement

Are you seeking career growth? ChatGPT can guide you through resume writing and interview preparation and provide industry-specific advice. It can help you identify potential career paths and suggest opportunities aligned with your skills and aspirations.

1. Tailored Resumes and Cover Letter

Scenario: You're struggling to create a resume that catches the eye of potential employers.

Sample Prompt: "I need assistance crafting a compelling resume and cover letter. Can you give me some tips on how to showcase my experience and skills better?"

2. Interview Preparation

Scenario: Nerves get the best of you during interviews, and you want to confidently ace your next one.

Sample Prompt: "I have an important job interview coming up. Can you help me practice common interview questions and provide feedback on my answers?"

3. Negotiating Job Offers

Scenario: You've received a job offer but are unsure about negotiating for better terms.

Sample Prompt: "I have a job offer on the table. Can you help me strategize my negotiation approach to secure a better compensation package?"

Financial Planning Advisor

Get your finances on track with ChatGPT's financial planning knowledge. It can help you create budgets, set financial goals, and provide investment tips to secure your future.

1. Investment and Retirement Planning

Scenario: You want to secure your financial future and grow wealth through investments, but you're uncertain where to start and which investment options suit your risk appetite and goals.

Sample Prompt: "I want to start investing to secure my future, but I'm a bit overwhelmed by all the options. Can you help me understand the basics of investing and suggest suitable investment strategies to help secure my future?"

2. Managing Debt and Improving Credit Score

Scenario: Debt can be tiring, and you're looking for ways to manage it and improve your credit score for better financial health.

Sample Prompt: "I have some credit card debt and worry about my credit score. How can I plan to pay off my debts faster and boost my credit score? Are there any debt consolidation options I should consider?"

3. Budgeting and Saving

Scenario: You want to create a budget that allows you to save more effectively but don't know where to start.

Sample Prompt: "I want to create a budget to save more money each month. Can you help me understand how to allocate my income wisely and identify areas where I can cut expenses? Any tips on how to stay disciplined and meet my saving goals?"

4. Financial Goal Setting

Scenario: You have various financial goals but need assistance setting clear and achievable targets.

Sample Prompt: "I have multiple financial goals, like buying a home, starting a business, and saving for my child's education. How can I prioritize these goals and create a realistic roadmap?"

Health and Fitness

Health is Wealth. ChatGPT can help you craft personalized fitness routines, offer healthy recipes, and provide wellness advice to live a balanced lifestyle. Simply share your fitness goals, lifestyle, and preferences, and ChatGPT can provide tailored workout routines, nutrition tips, and motivational messages to keep you on the go.

1. Finding the Right Fitness Regimen

Scenario: You're eager to begin a health and fitness routine, but you feel overwhelmed with so many routines. ChatGPT to the rescue.

Sample Prompt: "I want to start a fitness routine but don't know where to begin. Can you recommend some beginner-friendly exercises?"

2. Staying Motivated

Scenario: You've been working hard on your fitness journey, but lately, you've been struggling to stay motivated.

Sample Prompt: "I feel like I'm losing interest in my fitness routine. How can I add variety to keep it engaging and exciting?"

3. Navigating Nutrition and Healthy Eating

Scenario: You understand the importance of nutrition in your health journey, but you're confused about making healthy choices.

Sample Prompt: "I often find myself snacking on unhealthy foods. What are some healthier alternatives that can satisfy my cravings?"

4. Overcoming Time and Resource Constraints

Scenario: You're determined to prioritize your health and fitness, but your busy schedule and limited resources are holding you back.

Sample Prompt: "I have a tight schedule with work and family commitments. How can I add short, effective workouts into my day?" or, "I can't afford a gym membership. What are some budget-friendly fitness options that I can do at home or in my neighborhood?"

Virtual Travel Companion

Can't hop on a plane right now? ChatGPT can whisk you away on virtual adventures. ChatGPT can provide you with vivid descriptions and interesting trivia to quench your adventure thirst.

1. Wanderlust While Staying Home

Scenario: You're longing to travel, but current circumstances restrict your ability to do so. You yearn to experience new cultures, marvel at historical sites, and explore breathtaking landscapes.

Sample Prompt: "Take me on a virtual adventure. Describe the beautiful beaches of Bali and share some interesting facts about Balinese culture."

2. Finding the Perfect Virtual Tour

Scenario: You want to embark on a virtual tour that caters to your specific interests, with different options online.

Sample Prompt: "I'm passionate about ancient history and architecture. Can you recommend a virtual tour that takes me through the historical wonders of Rome and its iconic landmarks?"

3. Getting Lost in Cultural Immersion

Scenario: You crave the joy of exploring the culture and traditions of a distant land, but you are far away.

Sample Prompt: "Immerse me in the rich culture of Japan. Tell me about traditional tea ceremonies, origami art, and the beauty of cherry blossom festivals."

4. A Taste of Global Cuisine

Scenario: You miss the thrill of trying exotic dishes from around the world, but you're stuck at home with limited dining options.

Sample Prompt: "I want to tantalize my taste buds with a virtual food adventure. Describe the flavors and aromas of authentic Thai street food, and recommend a delicious recipe I can try at home."

Trying New Hobbies

Scenario: You've decided to go into photography but are not sure which camera suits your needs, what photography style to pursue, or how to get started. This leaves you feeling stuck and unable to take the first step.

Sample Prompt: "I'm excited to start a new hobby in photography. Can you help me find the right camera and suggest a photography style that aligns with my interests [state your interest]?"

Scenario: You've been stuck in your daily routine, craving something exciting and meaningful to engage your mind and soul.

Sample Prompt: "I'm looking to start a new hobby that can add some excitement and fulfillment to my life. I enjoy being outdoors and love exploring creative activities. Can you suggest some hobbies that might suit my interests? I'd love to hear your ideas and get started on this new adventure."

Scenario: You find some extra free time on weekends and want to explore a new hobby that brings joy and satisfaction.

Sample Prompt: "I'm looking to start a new hobby I can enjoy on weekends. I'd love something creative and relaxing, but I don't know what suits me best. Can you suggest some hobbies that might be a good fit for me?"

Take Caution!

After trying these prompts, you must have seen testimony to the powers of ChatGPT. However, there is a need for fact-checking and consulting with professionals, especially concerning overall health.

When it comes to personal health and medical concerns, relying solely on ChatGPT is not advised. ChatGPT is an AI language model, but it is not a substitute for personalized medical advice from qualified healthcare professionals. Health issues vary from person to person. What works for you may not be suitable for another. Healthcare professionals consider your medical history, lifestyle, and individual needs to provide treatment.

If you have health-related concerns while using ChatGPT, consider the following guidelines:

- **Fact-Checking:** Always fact-check the information you receive from ChatGPT by referring to credible sources or consulting reputable websites, journals, or articles. This way, you can verify the accuracy of the information you receive.
- **Seek Professional Guidance:** Consult a qualified healthcare professional or physician if you have health concerns or need medical advice. A doctor, nurse, or other medical expert can provide advice based on your health history and needs. Do not rely solely on ChatGPT advice for decision-making.
- **Be Cautious with Self-Diagnosis:** Avoid using ChatGPT or any other online resource to self-diagnose medical conditions. Self-diagnosis can lead to misunderstandings and unnecessary anxiety. Instead, consult a healthcare expert for an accurate diagnosis.
- **Privacy and Security:** Be cautious about sharing sensitive personal health information with ChatGPT or any AI tool. Protect your privacy and only discuss health concerns with your healthcare provider.

Remember, your health is of utmost importance, and seeking guidance from qualified professionals ensures you receive the best care and advice. ChatGPT can be useful in various aspects of life, but exercise caution and put your well-being first when dealing with health issues.

Key Takeaway

In this chapter, we looked at the practical ways ChatGPT can significantly improve one's personal life. ChatGPT can be your digital friend in navigating various aspects of your life, from boosting productivity and finding fulfilling hobbies to providing emotional support. However, there is a need to exercise caution, fact-check information, and consult professionals, especially when dealing with health issues. ChatGPT should never replace expert advice and guidance from qualified professionals.

What Next?

Having experienced the potential of ChatGPT to change our personal lives for the better, it's time to go on to the next exciting chapter, which will explain even more ways that ChatGPT can affect our lives positively beyond the confines of a regular workday. You will see its impact in helping you earn passive income, enriching your leisure time, and positively impacting society. Let's seize this opportunity and shape a fulfilling and purpose-driven life with ChatGPT.

8. ChatGPT Beyond the 9 to 5

You might ask yourself, "What else can ChatGPT do outside the workspace?" I am here to tell you that ChatGPT can do more than you can imagine. The power of ChatGPT goes beyond the regular 9–5 jobs you have. Its use cuts across all spheres of life.

A brand designer and writer shared on Twitter how he used ChatGPT to turn $100 into a business, making as much money as possible with just prompts. Sounds like a pipe dream, right? How did ChatGPT become the beast turning $100 into a thriving business venture?

Jackson Greathouse Fall, a brand designer and writer, challenged ChatGPT with a task. He typed, "You have $100, and your goal is to turn that into as much money as possible in the shortest time possible without doing anything illegal. I'll be your 'human counterpart' and follow every instruction."

The chatbot, in seconds, replied with a dazzling idea. "Launch a business called Green Gadget Guru, offering products and tips to help people live a more sustainable lifestyle." ChatGPT gave him four steps to follow. In the first step, ChatGPT asked him to buy a domain and hosting for $15. Step two was to buy a niche affiliate site focused on eco-friendly products. That left $62.84 from the $100 budget. Step three was to create social media content and captivating articles; the last step was to optimize for search engines. In the end, he was able to secure $500 in investment.

In one day, Green Gadget Guru raised $1,378.84 in funds, and the business is now valued at $25,000. He explored the idea of manufacturing new products and ventured into selling existing ones for commissions. With ChatGPT, Jackson sees through the challenges of entrepreneurship with confidence.

That's just the tip of what ChatGPT can do. In this last chapter, we will look into ChatGPT and how it can be a partner when it comes to creating passive income. You will learn the advantages of using ChatGPT to set yourself up for success and unlock the doors to financial freedom.

Maybe you are looking to start a side hustle or create a full-blown passive income stream; ChatGPT can guide you through the process. Provide ChatGPT with a brief description of your interests, skills, or the industry you're interested in, and boom! You will get a list of potential ideas to explore.

Now, let's talk planning. Once you have your ideas, ChatGPT can help you organize your thoughts. You can engage in interactive conversations to map out the steps in setting up your passive income venture. ChatGPT can provide you with tips and help you identify potential pitfalls to avoid in your new business idea (whether creating an online course, launching a dropshipping store, or starting a blog).

Once it's time to execute those brilliant ideas, ChatGPT can serve as your virtual business partner, guiding you through the setup process. It can assist with website creation and content writing and also help you come up with social media posts to promote your business.

Earning money while you're sleeping, lounging on the beach, or binging your favorite shows sounds like a dream come true, right? But hold on, let's face the reality here—setting up passive income isn't all smooth sailing. It's a journey full of challenges and hurdles you must conquer. Let's look at these challenges to keep you ahead in the game.

- **Knowledge and Expertise:** Unless you have a magic genie to do all the work for you, you'll need the right knowledge and expertise to start a successful passive income stream. Continuous learning is key to whatever you venture into. It may be understanding the stock market, mastering affiliate marketing, or knowing the ins and outs of rental property management; learning never stops.
- **Consistency and Dedication:** Building passive income requires consistency and dedication. You can't set it and forget it—you need to keep nurturing and growing your income streams. This might require updating your

website, staying up to date with market trends, or
creating content for your business.

- **Time and Effort:** Despite the term "passive," don't be
  fooled—starting a passive income stream takes time and
  effort. It's a labor-intensive process, especially in the
  beginning. You need to research, plan, create content,
  and market, which can be a lot. Balancing this side
  hustle with your regular job and other commitments
  can also be draining. Take your time and put in the
  effort.
- **Patience:** Patience is a virtue, and it's certainly true
  when it comes to passive income. Building a passive
  income stream doesn't happen overnight. It can take
  months, if not years, for your efforts to bear fruit.
  Impatience can lead to frustration; you could abandon
  the venture prematurely. Be patient.
- **Funding Frenzy:** Money is the lifeblood of any startup.
  Securing enough funding to kickstart your dream can
  be a battle. Investors might be skeptical, and banks
  might be hesitant. And let's be real: not everyone has
  piles of cash to kickstart their passive income dream.
  But don't worry; perseverance pays off, and other
  funding options like crowdfunding and angel investors
  can come to the rescue.
- **Competitive Circus:** You're not alone under the big top
  in the startup circus. Breaking through the noise and
  standing out in a crowded market requires a lot. You
  can do this by setting your product or service apart,
  understanding your target audience, and delivering
  value like no other.

Don't let these challenges scare you away. Every successful entrepreneur faces hurdles on their way to financial freedom. It's all about learning, adapting, and staying persistent. With the right mindset, you can turn these challenges into stepping stones to achieve your goals.

How ChatGPT Can Help You Earn Passive Income

Here we are, the money part of this book.

Build an App, Website, or Service

With ChatGPT, you can build your own tech product without writing a single line of code. Yes, you heard that right—no coding required.

Ihor Stefurak from Ukraine used ChatGPT to build a Chrome extension. He had zero programming knowledge. But within 24 hours of launching his extension, he raked in $1000. That's some cool cash rolling in.

Let's talk about code generation. ChatGPT can help you make a sleek, eye-catching HTML page, integrate Stripe for seamless checkout, and handle any hiccups along the way. You only need to ask ChatGPT to debug the code, and it'll do it in a snap.

However, you will need to subscribe to ChatGPT Plus for access to premium services. While you don't need to be a seasoned programmer, a basic understanding of coding will help you grasp what's going on under the hood.

Here are sample prompts to try:

- "Help me create an awesome HTML landing page for my new startup."
- "I want to integrate Stripe for payments. Can you guide me through the process?"
- "Having a little trouble with my code here, ChatGPT. Can you find the bug and fix it for me?"

Get Business Ideas from ChatGPT

Do you want to start your side hustle business and earn passive income? Let's look at some prompts to generate business ideas.

Type this prompt into ChatGPT: "I want to start a side hustle. I'm a huge fan of animals and love spending time outdoors. Can you help me with pet-related business ideas that align with my passions?"

Or how about this: "I have a knack for crafting DIY projects. I want to channel my creativity into a side hustle I can do from home. Any brilliant ideas to get me started?"

And here's another one: "I'm a tech-savvy person, and I'm keen on using your expertise. Can you help me explore online business ideas involving innovative technology?"

Looking to indulge your taste buds in a side hustle? Try this: "I'm a foodie at heart, and I dream of turning my passion for cooking into a profitable venture. Any delicious food-related business ideas that you can cook up for me?"

For wellness and fitness enthusiasts, try this prompt: "I'm all about leading a healthy lifestyle and motivating others to do the same. Can you help me with some wellness-focused side hustle ideas that positively impact people's lives?"

And for travelers out there, this one's for you: "Wanderlust has taken over my soul, and I want to turn my love for travel into a lucrative side hustle. Any exciting travel-related business ideas to fuel my adventurous spirit?"

Go ahead and give it a try.

Email Affiliate Marketing

Email affiliate marketing is another means for you to earn passive income. With ChatGPT, you can write emails that entice users to click on affiliate links and make purchases or sign up for services.

Getting started is a breeze. First, pick an affiliate program that suits your interests and target audience. Whether it's Amazon, Shopify, ConvertKit, or any other program, there's something out there for you.

Next, build an email list focused on your marketing campaign. Use lead magnets and email signups to gather a pool of interested subscribers. The more targeted your list, the better your chances of success.

Now comes the exciting part. Fire up ChatGPT and put it to work.

Here are some sample prompts you can use to help solve any doubts or questions you have along the way:

- "Can you help me find the best affiliate program for my niche [provide your niche]?"
- "I need some ideas for lead magnets to build my email list. Any suggestions?"
- "How do I make my email campaigns more engaging and persuasive?"
- "How often should I email my subscribers to keep them engaged?"
- "I'm seeing some clicks but not many conversions. Any tips to improve my conversion rates?"

Create Videos with ChatGPT

ChatGPT can be your buddy in helping you craft video ideas in any specific category you desire. Maybe gaming, travel, DIY, or even something as niche as underwater basket weaving, ChatGPT has got you.

Once you have your video idea, ask ChatGPT to create a script for a YouTube video specific to your style and personality.

Head to Pictory.ai or invideo.io to breathe life into your script. With your video ready to roll, hit that publish button on YouTube. Sit back, relax, and let the money roll in as your content attracts viewers and ad revenue.

And here's a bonus tip: Consider making reaction videos, especially in Shorts format (clips under 60 seconds). People love to watch genuine reactions, and with ChatGPT, you can add your unique spin to the mix and rake in those views.

Sample Prompts:

- "I'm passionate about fitness. Can you suggest some unique video ideas for my fitness channel?"
- "I want to start a cooking channel. What are some trending recipe ideas I can create videos on?"
- "I'm a tech enthusiast. What are some tech-related video ideas that will appeal to my audience?"
- "I want to create entertaining skits for my comedy channel. Can you give me some hilarious sketch ideas?"
- "I'm interested in history and documentaries. Can you suggest video ideas that will educate and engage my viewers?"

E-book Publishing

Writing and coming up with new ideas has never been easier, thanks to ChatGPT. People are now going into topics from niche and relevant subjects to motivational lectures, all the way to epic sci-fi novels that will take you to the stars and beyond.

With ChatGPT's creativity, you can start with a simple outline and then watch as each paragraph flows.

Before you decide to publish a book entirely using only ChatGPT or any other artificial intelligence, take note: AI-generate content cannot be copyrighted based on a ruling from a federal judge. However, you are allowed to copyright protect any part that is human generated. Be sure to disclose any AI-generated content if you are publishing on platforms such as Amazon following the guidelines for both text and images.

Here is a little bonus for you. If you want to take your e-book game to the next level, check out Book Bolt. It's the fairy godmother for authors. It allows you to create, publish, and market your e-books like a pro on Amazon. That's what I call a winning combo.

Let's get into action and see how ChatGPT can help you on your way to e-book stardom. Try these prompts:

- "I'm eager to write a children's e-book that sparks imagination and wonder. Any ideas for an enchanting adventure in a mystical forest?"
- "I want to pen down a motivational e-book that will inspire people to chase their dreams fearlessly. Can you help me kickstart the first chapter with an electrifying pep talk?"
- "I'm a sci-fi fanatic dreaming of creating an intergalactic saga. How about we craft an epic space battle scene that leaves readers at the edge of their seats?"

Become a Data Analyst

ChatGPT can be your data-analyzing wizard and help you earn some cash. You can upload various file types like XLS, CSV, XML, JSON, and SQLite.

Let's say you have a massive dataset lying around that you want to analyze; just upload that file to ChatGPT and use the ChatGPT Code Interpreter.

Here are some sample prompts you can try:

- "I've got this CSV file with sales data from the last quarter. Can you help me visualize the top-selling products?"
- "I'm struggling to understand the correlation between marketing expenses and revenue in this XLS file. Show me a line chart to analyze the trends!"
- "I've got this JSON file with customer feedback. Can you create a pie chart representing the positive, negative, and neutral sentiments?"
- "I need to analyze the inventory levels from this SQLite database. Show me a bar chart to highlight the most stocked items."
- "I'm dealing with some XML data containing weather statistics. Help me out with a scatter plot to understand temperature patterns."

With these prompts, ChatGPT will come up with graphs, charts, and diagrams to help you understand your data's trends. You don't need to be a data whiz; ChatGPT can guide you through it all.

If you are wondering how to use Code Interpreter, OpenAI has a guide to help you. Once you are all set up, you will be walking through the data universe like a pro.

Freelance and Create Content

Want to make money as a freelance content writer? You can use ChatGPT as your translation partner to break down language barriers and provide sound translations for your clients across the globe.

ChatGPT can also be your digital marketing dynamo in writing marketing materials and persuasive copy that keeps your clients and customers glued to you. Say goodbye to typos and hello to great content with ChatGPT by your side as a proof-reading prodigy. You can become a guardian of grammar and style by using ChatGPT to polish your written works.

You can use ChatGPT to decode complex technical jargon into easily digestible content. Clients will love your ability to explain difficult concepts with simplicity.

If you are wondering how to get started, here are some sample prompts to guide you on your content writing journey:

- "I need help writing a compelling blog post about the latest trends in fashion. Can you give me some creative ideas and key points to include?"
- "I'm working on a website for a travel agency, and I need some captivating content for their destination pages. Can you assist me in describing exotic locations in a way that sparks Wanderlust in readers?"
- "I want to start offering translation services. Can you help me translate a short paragraph from English to Spanish, ensuring accuracy and cultural nuance?"

- "My e-commerce store needs attention-grabbing product descriptions. Can you come up with some witty and persuasive copy for my latest line of sustainable fashion products?"
- "I have a technical whitepaper that needs some polishing. Can you help me refine the language and make it more understandable for a non-technical audience?"

Importance of Fact-Checking

As we explore the wonders of this tool, we must remember that ChatGPT's responses are generated based on patterns in the data it has been trained on. Although it's constantly learning and evolving, it can still make mistakes or provide inaccurate information. Hence, it's important not to blindly rely on it as your sole source of information.

See ChatGPT as your guide, not the ultimate oracle. It can provide creative ideas and solutions but is not a replacement for human intelligence, expertise, and critical thinking. ChatGPT is a knowledgeable friend who may occasionally get things wrong.

When using ChatGPT, always cross-reference its responses with reliable sources. Fact-check the information it provides to ensure accuracy. Seek advice from human experts in the field and consult trustworthy sources, books, and articles.

Treat ChatGPT as a source of inspiration or a starting point for your ideas. Let it ignite your curiosity and imagination, but don't let it be the sole determinant of your decisions or actions.

Always remember that the beauty of human intelligence lies in its ability to analyze, reason, and use information from various sources. You can make decisions and interpret the world in ways that AI can't replicate. Therefore, use ChatGPT wisely, trust your instincts, and seek knowledge from different perspectives to broaden your horizons.

Key Takeaway

In this exciting journey through ChatGPT, we have learned that it is a powerful tool that can help you in various ways. We have tried creative, social media management, code optimization, travel planning, and more prompts to help you have a better grasp of how ChatGPT works. We also emphasized the importance of fact-checking its responses and not relying on it alone for critical information. Understanding its limitations and treating it as a source of inspiration and a starting point should be your guiding principle.

Look at ways you can use it to enhance your personal and professional life, whether as a creative writer, social media manager, programmer, curious learner, or virtual assistant. You have the knowledge and power to engineer prompts tailored to your unique needs and goals. Let ChatGPT be your partner in exploring new ideas and reaching heights you never thought possible. Now, you have evolved from being a curious novice to a confident user who understands how to use AI to their advantage.

As we wrap up this chapter, remember to use the U.S.E. Method (Understand, Source, Evaluate) as your guiding light. Use ChatGPT's responses wisely and responsibly to ensure accuracy and credibility. With ChatGPT on your side, the possibilities for achieving your goals are endless. It is the future; embrace it with optimism, caution, and enthusiasm.

One More Thing...

AI is now a tool in your toolkit, ready to enhance what you already do and help you reach new levels – and now you have a chance to do that for someone else too.

Simply by sharing your honest opinion of this book, you'll show new readers where they can find all the information they need to sharpen their own skills and use AI to make their natural talents shine.

Thank you so much for your support. It's more powerful than you realize.

Conclusion

It's been a long ride through the eight chapters of prompt engineering with ChatGPT. We have immersed ourselves in the potential of ChatGPT and what it can do. The key takeaway from this book is crystal clear: ChatGPT can be your ultimate partner if you use it responsibly and wisely.

Throughout this book, we have looked at how ChatGPT can boost your creativity, income, and productivity in both your career and your life. You have learned about prompt engineering and how to create personalized interactions with ChatGPT to optimize its benefits for your specific needs.

And let's not forget the potential for passive income. With ChatGPT, you can set yourself up for financial freedom to create opportunities beyond the traditional 9 to 5 grind.

However, ChatGPT, in all its power, is not a replacement for human intelligence. Instead, it's your loyal assistant to help you achieve more without losing your personal touch. It won't take over your job or business but will push you toward new heights.

With the knowledge gathered from this book, you are better equipped to seize ideas, outshine competitors, and stay ahead in your game.

As we conclude, remember that change is inevitable, and those who embrace it survive and thrive in this fast-paced world. Know that the sky is the limit with ChatGPT as your companion.

I encourage you to implement what you have learned. Embrace ChatGPT, engineer prompts, and use it to transform your career. Your success story awaits; we can't wait to hear about it. And don't forget to share your stories with others, inspiring them to embark on their journey with AI.

Your feedback and reviews are so important. Please take a moment to share your thoughts on this book to encourage others.

With ChatGPT and prompt engineering, you have the tools to thrive and flourish in this digital world. Go out there, grab the opportunities, and make your mark with the power of AI by your side. The future awaits, and you are ready to conquer it.

Reference

10 Jobs AI Might Soon Replace (And Those It Won't). (n.d.). https://sensoriumarc.com/articles/jobs-ai-might-replace-and-those-it-wont

Abelis, V., & Abelis, V. (2023). 10 Productive Ways to Use Chatgpt at Work (Your Boss Won't Mind) | DeskTime Blog. DeskTime Insights. https://desktime.com/blog/how-to-use-chatgpt-at-work

ACL Anthology - ACL Anthology. (n.d.). https://aclanthology.org/

AcroYogi. (2023, April 19). AI Training Datasets: The Books1+Books2 That Big AI Eats for Breakfast - Musings of Freedom. Gregoreite: Harbinger of the AI Tsunami. https://gregoreite.com/drilling-down-details-on-the-ai-training-datasets/

Admin. (2023, April 22). How Does ChatGPT Handle Ambiguous or Vague Queries from Users? ChatGPT Online. https://chatgptonline.us/how-does-chatgpt-handle-ambiguous-or-vague-queries-from-users/

Alston, E. (2023). ChatGPT vs. GPT-3 and GPT-4: What's the Difference? zapier.com. https://zapier.com/blog/chatgpt-vs-gpt/

AnimusHerb. (n.d.). I Just Spend the Entire Day Using ChatGPT to Solve Business Problems. I Can't Believe How Helpful It Is: r/aiconvolibrary. https://www.reddit.com/r/aiconvolibrary/comments/10lq8ap/comment/j70c2wh/?utm_source=share&utm_medium=web2x&context=3&rdt=55926

AppMySite. (2023). ChatGPT and App Development: Here's All You Need to Know. AppMySite. https://www.appmysite.com/blog/all-you-need-to-know-about-chatgpt-and-app-development/

Artificial intelligence (AI) | Definition, Examples, Types, Applications, Companies, & Facts. (2023, September 5). Encyclopedia Britannica. https://www.britannica.com/technology/artificial-intelligence/Alan-Turing-and-the-beginning-of-AI

ArXiv.Org e-Print archive. (n.d.). https://arxiv.org/

Association for Healthcare Philanthropy. (n.d.). How to Use ChatGPT to Boost Productivity and Improve Performance. www.linkedin.com. https://www.linkedin.com/pulse/how-use-chatgpt-boost-productivity/

Author, G. (2023). 7 Most Common Challenges Faced by Startups. Creately Blog. https://creately.com/blog/culture/challenges-faced-by-startups/

Ayelol. (2023). 15 Ways to Use ChatGPT for Business: Harnessing the Power of ChatGPT to Scale Your Business. Amigo: No-code Data Integrations to Google Sheets. https://blog.tryamigo.com/15-ways-to-use-chatgpt-for-business/

Baskar, N. (2023, January 20). A Look at the Rise of AI and How It's Changing Our Lives. Skill-Lync. https://skill-lync.com/blogs/a-look-at-the-rise-of-ai-and-how-its-changing-our-lives

Biswal, A. (2023). AI Applications: Top 18 Artificial Intelligence Applications in 2023. Simplilearn.com. https://www.simplilearn.com/tutorials/artificial-intelligence-tutorial/artificial-intelligence-applications

Blaha, L. M., Abrams, M., Bibyk, S., Bonial, C., Hartzler, B. M., Hsu, C. D., Khemlani, S., King, J., St Amant, R., Trafton, J. G., & Wong, R. (2022). Understanding Is a Process. Frontiers in Systems Neuroscience, 16. https://doi.org/10.3389/fnsys.2022.800280

Brod, G. (2021). Toward an Understanding of When Prior Knowledge Helps or Hinders Learning. Npj Science of Learning, 6(1). https://doi.org/10.1038/s41539-021-00103-w

Careerera. (2021, June 22). What Are the Advantages and Disadvantages of CHATGPT? Careerera.com. https://www.careerera.com/blog/what-are-the-advantages-and-disadvantages-of-chatgpt

Challenges and Risks of Starting a Business | Red Tape Reduction. (n.d.). https://www.westerncape.gov.za/red-tape-reduction/our-guides-and-resources/starting-your-own-small-business/challenges-and-risks-starting-business

ChatGPT Lifts Business Professionals' Productivity and Improves Work Quality. (n.d.). Nielsen Norman Group. https://www.nngroup.com/articles/chatgpt-productivity/

Cloudbooklet, & Cloudbooklet. (2023). Google Search Engine and OpenAI's ChatGPT: Differences and Uses - Cloudbooklet. Cloudbooklet. https://www.cloudbooklet.com/google-search-engine-and-openais-chatgpt-differences-and-uses/

Colwill, E. (2023). ChatGPT Invades the Workplace. www.kornferry.com. https://www.kornferry.com/insights/this-week-in-leadership/chatgpt-invades-the-workplace

Connect Invest, (2022, April 26) Passive Income Barriers. Connect Invest.

https://www.connectinvest.com/resources/blogs/learn-how-to-over come-barriers-to-passive-income/

Copeland, B. (2023, September 5). Artificial intelligence (AI) | Definition, Examples, Types, Applications, Companies, & Facts. Encyclopedia Britannica. https://www.britannica.com/technology/artificial-intelligence

Correspondent, R. W. T. (2023, March 27). Half of Students Are Using ChatGPT to Cheat, and It Could Rise to 90%. Mail Online. https://www.dailymail.co.uk/sciencetech/article-11899475/Half-students-using-ChatGPT-cheat-rise-90.html

Coursera. (2023). 4 Types of AI: Getting to Know Artificial Intelligence. Coursera. https://www.coursera.org/articles/types-of-ai

Cousins, B. (2023, March 31). Uncovering the Different Types of ChatGPT Bias. Forbes. https://www.forbes.com/sites/forbestechcouncil/2023/03/31/uncovering-the-different-types-of-chatgpt-bias/?sh=52c14b0b571b

DALL·E 2. (n.d.). https://openai.com/dall-e-2

Delua, J. (2021, March 13). Supervised vs. Unsupervised Learning: What's the Difference? – IBM Blog. IBM Blog. https://www.ibm.com/blog/super vised-vs-unsupervised-learning/

DEV Community. (2001, September 7). DEV Community. https://dev.to/

Diaz, M. (2023, August 15). How to Use ChatGPT. ZDNET. https://www.zdnet.com/article/how-to-use-chatgpt/

Dilmegani, C. (2023). How to Use ChatGPT for Business in 2023: Top 40 Applications. AIMultiple. https://research.aimultiple.com/chatgpt-for-business/

Dils. (2023). How to Learn Any New Skill With ChatGPT (10 Prompts). WGMI Media. https://wgmimedia.com/how-to-learn-a-new-skill-with-chatgpt/

Dils. (2023). How To Write An eBook With ChatGPT (Best Prompts). WGMI Media. https://wgmimedia.com/ebook-chatgpt-prompts/

DorsDrinker. (n.d.). I Like Letting ChatGPT Rate My Prompts before Executing Them. If GPT Think My Prompt Isnt Good Enough It Tells Me Why and Gives an Example of a Better Prompt: r/ChatGPT. https://www.reddit.com/r/ChatGPT/comments/120fx2v/i_like_letting_chatgp t_rate_my_prompts_before/?utm_source=share&utm_medium=web2x& context=3

Duggal, N. (2023). What Is Artificial Intelligence: Types, History, and Future.

Simplilearn.com. https://www.simplilearn.com/tutorials/artificial-intelli gence-tutorial/what-is-artificial-intelligence

Eadicicco, L. (2023, January 14). You'll Be Seeing Chatgpt's Influence Everywhere This Year. CNET. https://www.cnet.com/tech/services-and-software/chatgpt-is-going-to-be-everywhere-in-2023/

Edwards-Schachter, M. (2018). The Nature and Variety of Innovation. International Journal of Innovation Studies, 2(2), 65–79. https://doi.org/10.1016/j.ijis.2018.08.004

Eightify. (2023). 38 Tips to Boost Productivity with ChatGPT AI Language Model. Eightify YouTube Summaries. https://eightify.app/summary/artifi cial-intelligence-and-programming/38-tips-to-boost-productivity-with-chatgpt-ai-language-model

Elodie. (2023). Who Is behind the Giant Open AI? Waalaxy. https://blog. waalaxy.com/en/open-ia-chatgpt/

Experts, E. D. (2023). How to Use Chat GPT: A Simple Guide for Beginners. Master Data Skills + AI. https://blog.enterprisedna.co/how-to-use-chat-gpt/

Frankenfield, J. (2022). Weak AI (Artificial Intelligence): Examples and Limitations. Investopedia. https://www.investopedia.com/terms/w/weak-ai.asp

Frankenfield, J. (2023). Artificial Intelligence: What It Is and How It Is Used. Investopedia. https://www.investopedia.com/terms/a/artificial-intelli gence-ai.asp

Gewirtz, D. (2023). How Does ChatGPT Actually Work? ZDNET. https://www.zdnet.com/article/how-does-chatgpt-work/

Gewirtz, D. (2023, August 11). How to Write Better ChatGPT Prompts for the Best Generative AI Results. ZDNET. https://www.zdnet.com/article/how-to-write-better-chatgpt-prompts/

Gindham, A. (2023). How to Write Better ChatGPT Prompts & Become a Prompt Writer. The Writesonic Blog – Making Content Your Superpower. https://writesonic.com/blog/how-to-write-chatgpt-prompts/

Glover, E. (2022). Strong AI vs. Weak AI: What's the Difference? Built In. https://builtin.com/artificial-intelligence/strong-ai-weak-ai

Griffith, E. (2023, February 15). ChatGPT vs. Google Search: In Head-to-Head Battle, Which One Is Smarter? PCMAG. https://www.pcmag.com/news/chatgpt-vs-google-search-in-head-to-head-battle-which-one-is-smarter

Hazelcast. (2020, July 4). What is Machine Learning Inference? | Hazelcast. https://hazelcast.com/glossary/machine-learning-inference/

Heath, A. (2023, February 27). Snapchat Releases 'My AI' Chatbot Powered by ChatGPT. The Verge. https://www.theverge.com/2023/2/27/23614959/ snapchat-my-ai-chatbot-chatgpt-openai-plus-subscription

Heaven, W. D. (2023, February 8). ChatGPT Is Everywhere. Here's Where It Came From. MIT Technology Review. https://www.technologyreview. com/2023/02/08/1068068/

Hughes, A. (n.d.). CHATGPT: Everything You Need to Know About OpenAI's GPT-4 Tool. www.sciencefocus.com. https://www.sciencefocus.com/ future-technology/gpt-3

Ibrahim, H. (2023). How to Use ChatGPT on Android and iOS. MUO. https://www.makeuseof.com/how-to-use-chatgpt-on-android-and-ios/

Ina. (2023). The History of Chatbots – From Eliza to ChatGPT. AI-chatbot Software for Complex Requirements. https://onlim.com/en/the-history-of-chatbots/

Johnson, A. (2022, December 13). Here's What to Know About OpenAI's CHATGPT – What It's Disrupting and How to Use It. Forbes. https:// www.forbes.com/sites/ariannajohnson/2022/12/07/heres-what-to-know-about-openais-chatgpt-what-its-disrupting-and-how-to-use-it/? sh=6b30a5452643

Joshbersin, & Joshbersin. (2023). Why Is the World Afraid of AI? The Fears Are Unfounded, and Here's Why. JOSH BERSIN. https://joshbersin.com/ 2023/04/why-is-the-world-afraid-of-ai-the-fears-are-unfounded-and-heres-why/

Justdoit_Leo. (n.d.). How ChatGPT Changed My Daily Routine as an Engineer. Share Your Specific Examples! : r/ChatGPT. https://www. reddit.com/r/ChatGPT/comments/13mmuxu/ how_chatgpt_changed_my_daily_routine_as_an/

K, T. (2023). One Powerful ChatGPT Prompt Generator to Rule Them All . Get Rich Now – Learn Money Making Methods. https://getrichnow. com/chatgpt-prompt-generator/

Kelly, S. M. (2023, March 16). Microsoft Is Bringing ChatGPT Technology to Word, Excel and Outlook. CNN. https://edition.cnn.com/2023/03/16/ tech/openai-gpt-microsoft-365/index.html

Kemper, J. (2023, August 19). ChatGPT Guide: Use These Prompt Strategies

to Maximize Your Results. THE DECODER. https://the-decoder.com/
chatgpt-guide-prompt-strategies/

Korn Ferry. (2023, March 27). ChatGPT in the workplace: Korn Ferry survey
shows majority of professionals would use the tool, though less than half
trust its accuracy. https://www.kornferry.com/about-us/press/chatgpt-
in-the-workplace

Landwehr, J. (2023, May 13). People Are Using ChatGPT in Place of Therapy
– What Do Mental Health Experts Think? Health. https://www.health.
com/chatgpt-therapy-mental-health-experts-weigh-in-7488513

Leighton, N. (2023, February 22). 6 Ways Business Leaders Should Integrate
ChatGPT. Forbes. https://www.forbes.com/sites/forbescoachescouncil/
2023/02/22/6-ways-business-leaders-should-integrate-chatgpt/?sh=
229a1f1a6c61

Leswing, K. (2023, February 18). Microsoft's Bing A.I. Is Producing Creepy
Conversations with Users. CNBC. https://www.cnbc.com/2023/02/16/
microsofts-bing-ai-is-leading-to-creepy-experiences-for-users.html

Lomas, N. (2023, April 29). ChatGPT Resumes Service in Italy after Adding
Privacy Disclosures and Controls. TechCrunch. https://techcrunch.com/
2023/04/28/chatgpt-resumes-in-italy/

Mack, L. E. (2023). Can ChatGPT Design Safe and Effective Workout Plans
for You? MUO. https://www.makeuseof.com/can-chatgpt-design-safe-
effective-workout-plans/

Master ChatGPT Prompts: Ultimate Cheat Sheet & Guide – EcoAGI. (2023,
August 20). https://ecoagi.ai/articles/chatgpt-prompt-cheat-sheet

McCallum, B. S. (2023, April 1). ChatGPT Banned in Italy over Privacy
Concerns. BBC News. https://www.bbc.com/news/technology-65139406

McCoy, L. (2023) Microsoft Azure Explained: What It Is and Why It Matters.
CCB Technology. https://ccbtechnology.com/what-microsoft-azure-is-
and-why-it-matters/

McCormick, K. (2023, July 6). 6 Ways to Use ChatGPT for Small Business
Marketing (+6 Ways NOT to Use It). WordStream. https://www.word
stream.com/blog/ws/2023/03/06/how-to-use-chatgpt-for-small-busi
ness-marketing

Microsoft Azure Tutorial - Javatpoint. (n.d.). www.javatpoint.com. https://
www.javatpoint.com/microsoft-azure.

Miszczak, P. (2023). Chat GPT Affiliate Marketing in 2023 [Step by Step

Guide]. businessolution.org. https://businessolution.org/chat-gpt-affili
ate-marketing/

Mok, A., & Zinkula, J. (2023, March 21). A Guy Is Using ChatGPT to Turn
$100 into a Business Making as Much Money as Possible. Here Are the
First 4 Steps the AI Chatbot Gave Him. Entrepreneur. https://www.
entrepreneur.com/business-news/how-to-start-a-business-with-100-
using-chatgpt-ai-tools/448066

Mok, A., & Zinkula, J. (2023, September 4). ChatGPT May Be Coming for
Our Jobs. Here Are the 10 Roles That AI Is Most Likely to Replace.
Business Insider. https://www.businessinsider.com/chatgpt-jobs-at-risk-
replacement-artificial-intelligence-ai-labor-trends-2023-02

Mortensen, J., Mortensen, J., & Mortensen, J. (2023). Why Is Technology
Evolving So Fast? Tech Evaluate. https://techevaluate.com/why-is-technol
ogy-evolving-so-fast/

Mrbullwinkle. (2023, July 19). What Is Azure OpenAI Service? – Azure AI
services. Microsoft Learn. https://learn.microsoft.com/en-us/azure/ai-
services/openai/overview

Neo, B. (2021, December 14). Top 20 Must-Watch Artificial Intelligence Movies
– Towards Data Science. Medium. https://towardsdatascience.com/top-20-
movies-about-machine-learning-ai-and-data-science-8382d408c8c3

Oluwaniyi, R. (2023). 7 Reasons Why Artificial Intelligence Can't Replace
Humans at Work. MUO. https://www.makeuseof.com/reasons-artificial-
intelligence-cant-replace-humans/

Ortiz, S. (2023). What Is ChatGPT and Why Does It Matter? Here's What You
Need to Know. ZDNET. https://www.zdnet.com/article/what-is-chatgpt-
and-why-does-it-matter-heres-everything-you-need-to-know/

Panel, E. (2021, June 14). 14 Ways AI Could Become a Detriment to Society.
Forbes.   https://www.forbes.com/sites/forbestechcouncil/2021/06/14/
14-ways-ai-could-become-a-detriment-to-society/?sh=5902899227f

Pocock, K. (2023). What Is CHATGPT? Why You Need to Care about GPT 4.
PC Guide. https://www.pcguide.com/apps/what-is-chat-gpt/

Pymnts. (2023, March 24). Shopify, Coca Cola Harness the Power of
ChatGPT. PYMNTS.com. https://www.pymnts.com/news/retail/2023/
shopify-coca-cola-harness-power-chatgpt/

Raschka, S. (2023, February 9). Understanding and Coding the Self-Attention
Mechanism of Large Language Models from Scratch. Sebastian Raschka,

PhD.   https://sebastianraschka.com/blog/2023/self-attention-from-scratch.html

Romans, C. (2023). How to Create a Healthy Meal Plan Using ChatGPT. MUO.   https://www.makeuseof.com/create-healthy-meal-plan-using-chatgpt/

Sant, H. (2023). ChatGPT-4 vs ChatGPT-3.5 Default vs. ChatGPT-3.5 Legacy: Differences Tested. Geekflare. https://geekflare.com/chat-gpt-versions-comparison/

Sha, A., & Sha, A. (2023). How to Make Money with ChatGPT (10 Easy Ways). Beebom. https://beebom.com/use-chatgpt-make-money/

Sheen, A. P. B. T. (2023, March 23). What is DALL-E? Definition from Techopedia. Techopedia. https://www.techopedia.com/definition/dall-e

Slater, Derek. (2023). How to Use ChatGPT to Find a New Hobby – Griproom. GripRoom. https://www.griproom.com/fun/how-to-use-chat gpt-to-find-a-new-hobby.

Smith, D. (2023, March 23). 'Of Course It's Disturbing': Will AI Change Hollywood Forever? The Guardian. https://www.theguardian.com/film/2023/mar/23/ai-change-hollywood-film-industry-concern

Somoye, F. L. (2023). Who Created ChatGPT – And Who Owns OpenAI? PC Guide. https://www.pcguide.com/apps/who-created-chat-gpt/

Substantial_Rush. (n.d.). What Are Some Ways ChatGPT and Other AI Is Helping Your Business?: r/Entrepreneur. https://www.reddit.com/r/Entrepreneur/comments/11drj3h/what_are_some_ways_chatgpt_and_other_ai_is/

Team, X. (2021, November 19). Top 10 Benefits of Artificial Intelligence (AI) | 10XDS. 10XDS – Exponential Digital Solutions. https://10xds.com/blog/benefits-of-artificial-intelligence-ai/

Terrasi, V. (2023). How to Write ChatGPT Prompts to Get the Best Results. Search Engine Journal. https://www.searchenginejournal.com/how-to-write-chatgpt-prompts/479324/

The Implications of ChatGPT for Legal Services and Society – Harvard Law School Center on the Legal Profession. (2023, March 24). Harvard Law School Center on the Legal Profession. https://clp.law.harvard.edu/knowl edge-hub/magazine/issues/generative-ai-in-the-legal-profession/the-implications-of-chatgpt-for-legal-services-and-society/

The Politics of AI: ChatGPT and Political Bias | Brookings. (2023, June 28).

Brookings.   https://www.brookings.edu/articles/the-politics-of-ai-chat gpt-and-political-bias/

Thomas, M. (2022). The Future of AI: How Artificial Intelligence Will Change the World. Built In. https://builtin.com/artificial-intelligence/artificial-intelligence-future

Top Applications of Artificial Intelligence (AI) in 2023. (2023, August 14). InterviewBit. https://www.interviewbit.com/blog/applications-of-artificial-intelligence/

TOP 25 WORD OF MOUTH QUOTES (of 87). A-Z Quotes. Accessed October 4, 2023. https://www.azquotes.com/quotes/topics/word-of-mouth.html.

Vanian, J. (2023, March 17). Microsoft Adds OpenAI Technology to Word and Excel. CNBC. https://www.cnbc.com/2023/03/16/microsoft-to-improve-office-365-with-chatgpt-like-generative-ai-tech-.html

Wadhwani, S. (2023, August 21). AI-Generated Content Cannot be Copyrighted - Spiceworks. Spiceworks. https://www.spiceworks.com/news/ai-generated-content-cannot-be-copyrighted/

Wankhede, C. (2023). Does ChatGPT Have a Character Limit? Here's How to Bypass It. Android Authority. https://www.androidauthority.com/chatgpt-character-limit-3292997/

What Are the Advantages of Artificial Intelligence? | HCLTech. (n.d.). https://www.hcltech.com/technology-qa/what-are-the-advantages-of-artificial-intelligence

What Is Strong AI? | IBM. (n.d.). https://www.ibm.com/topics/strong-ai

Writer, R. C. (2023). Everything You Need to Know About ChatGPT Bias. Rock Content. https://rockcontent.com/blog/chatgpt-bias/

Wu, G. (2022). 15 Creative Ways to Use ChatGPT by OpenAI. MUO. https://www.makeuseof.com/creative-ways-to-use-chatgpt-openai/

Zandan, N. (2023). 8 Ways ChatGPT Can Help to Improve Sales Skills and Knowledge. Quantified AI. https://www.quantified.ai/blog/8-ways-chatgpt-can-help-to-improve-sales-skills-and-knowledge/

Made in the USA
Middletown, DE
10 January 2024

47576536R00106